STREISAND

BOB DEUTSCH

THROUGH THE LENS

DEDICATION
To Joan Engels, Jim Kenney,
and the rest of the NEWSWEEK staff
for their loyalty.

STREISAND
THROUGH THE LENS

PHOTO-EDITED BY
FRANK TETI

WRITTEN BY
KAREN MOLINE

BOOK DESIGN: VIRGINIA RUBEL
FRONT COVER DESIGN: ED CARAEFF

A Delilah Book Distributed by The Putnam Publishing Group, New York

A Delilah Book

Delilah Communications Ltd.
118 E. 25 Street
New York, New York 10010

ISBN: 0-933328-42-7
Library of Congress Catalog Card Number: 82-71723

Manufactured in the U.S.A.
First printing 1982

ACKNOWLEDGMENTS

Special thanks to the following, without whose generous contributions this book would not have been possible: all the photographers in this book, Dallas, John Downey, George Haddad-Garcia, Karen Moline, Michel Parenteau, Neal Peters and David Smith, Jeannie Sakol, Sotheby's Belgravia, Frank A. Teti, and Lou Valentino.

My gratitude to all my friends for their support along the way: Tommy Allessio, Jamie Auchincloss, Vince Bantinelli, Arthur Bell, Jennie Bilotta, Bobbi Baker Burrows, Larry Cappello, Allan Carr, Julio Caesar Chacur, Eddie De La Rosa, Rhett Dennis, John Devere, Lynn Dorsey, Ann Durzita, Don Estes, Bob Fish, Freida, Gracie, Paula Greene, Alvin Grossman, Elinor Haber, Mr. and Mrs. Joe Hamilton, Andrea Henderson, Wayne Johnson, Gary Kalkan, Mr. and Mrs. Robert Kennedy, Peter Kersten, Steven Konigsberg, Leo Lerman, Eddie (fish tank) Marotta, Patty Mansy, Robbi Miller, Peter Murray, Bob Molinari, Patricia Newcomb, Nicky Nichols, Louis Perego, Tom Poster, David Ragan, Mr. and Mrs. Michael J. Rebis, Melody Miller Rogers, Emilio Rubia, Vito Russo, Steve Ryan, Mark Saffer, Dosie Salvatore, Jeff Sessa, Marc Paul Simon, Mel Scott, Marie Schumann, Stephen Smith, Mr. and Mrs. Roger Smith, Lois Webber Smith, Lee Solters, John Springer, Larry Thomas, John Thursh, Geri Ulrich, Jim Watters, and Jimmy Yaghy.

Special thanks, also, to Stephanie Bennett, Ed Caraeff, Amit Shah, Una Fahy, and Richard Schatzberg.

To all my family members, past and present, for their love and belief.

And finally to Barbra Streisand, whose great talents have brought myself and so many others, great joy.

STREISAND
THROUGH THE LENS

PHOTOGRAPHS AND INTERVIEWS WITH

CECIL BEATON
YANI BEGAKIS
BOB DEUTSCH
RON GALELLA
TONY RIZZO
SANTIAGO RODRIGUEZ
FRANK TETI

BOB SCOTT

CONTENTS

Introduction

STREISAND: THROUGH THE LENS is not a conventional biography about a celebrated movie star. It is, instead, a unique concept: an unabashed and candid look at one of the most talented, charismatic, unconventionally beautiful, and popular superstars of our time, as told by photographers who have "shot" her over the years. Their anecdotes, struggles, successes, and impressions comprise the text of this book.

For over twenty years, the photojournalists in THROUGH THE LENS have been professional Streisand observers. Their photographs have appeared in the pages and on the covers of every major magazine throughout the world. Most of these pictures have never been published or exhibited before. STREISAND: THROUGH THE LENS displays the photographers'—and public's—enduring fascination with Barbra Streisand.

Barbra Streisand may seem an unlikely subject for a book **by** photographers. Though she has been hailed as one of the great beauties of our age, she is notoriously camera-shy. Why? She's a superstar; what's another flashbulb. Yet as the interviews point out, the answer varies with the perceptions of each photographer, and the situation is paradoxically complex.

Perhaps, Barbra's dislike of being photographed stems from her adolescent insecurities about her appearance: how skinny she was, how her nose looked, her complexion. Yet

Streisand, secure about the strength of her talent, refused to have her nose fixed—though she was often advised to do so. Her decision was indeed wise, for it made her unforgettable. Who will forget the image of that famous profile, the long, elegant neck and fingernails, the immense eyes? She appeals to every audience; she has been on the covers of magazines from VOGUE to PLAYBOY, LIFE to LOOK, MODERN SCREEN to the NATIONAL ENQUIRER. She has been compared to the glorious beauties Nefertiti and Aphrodite, yet, at heart, she remains Barbra Streisand, from Brooklyn, New York.

And Barbra has something more: a style, a look of her own, an indescribable presence. She may often change her hairstyle but she never loses her character: when her hair was short and straight, parted on the side, gamine-like, it was Barbra; when frizzed à la Jon Peters, it was still Barbra. When she was on the Best and Worst Dressed list in the same year, Barbra again. She was wearing thrift shop clothes (partially out of necessity) and looking "kooky" long before the masses of hippies caught on to the idea. She dared to wear a see-through (and most said "highly unflattering") outfit to the Academy Awards ceremony. She exercised her firm derrière onscreen before Jane Fonda thought of her exercise salons. Barbra doesn't expect to be followed; her style is as much a part of her as that incredible voice.

Part of Streisand's appeal to photographers also lies in the fact that she makes it so difficult for anyone to take her picture. What is inaccessible is naturally more appealing, to say nothing of the lure of the challenge, the battle of wits. Streisand rarely goes out in public, she rarely poses in private; even at press functions she'll pose for the shortest time possible and then escape. Photographers need patience, perseverance, clever guesswork, and a lot of luck to catch a good shot. Why does she make it so difficult—especially for herself? Certainly Barbra must detest and be terrified of the mob scenes at premieres, the crowds outside a benefit. What is the charm of sneaking through the kitchen? Yet Barbra, even when she **knows** she is going to be photographed, even when surrounded by hordes of Nikons, in public, will **not** stop and pose. She will hide her face, run, grimace, turn around or have her escort try to protect her face. Is it stubborn pride, or fear, or anger and resentment that she cannot be left alone? If she so craves solitude, why has she chosen and continued in a profession which is dependent upon being in a perpetual limelight? And naturally, the shots that do appear after these harrowing sessions are not in the least flattering.

All the photographers I spoke to agreed—and some at great length—that Streisand avoids any situation where she is not in control. She has certain ideas about her appearance, and given her astounding success (her personal income for 1980 was over **twenty** million dollars), she can certainly afford to do what she wants. Barbra has always had strong ideas about her talent and style—and she's usually been right. She knows her audience, and her strengths as a singer and actress. With her latest project, YENTL, she is not only starring, but producing and directing as well: more control. Even on the rare occasion where she agrees to pose, she'll usually turn her head; she prefers her left profile. She obviously feels that she can afford to dictate to the public what she wants them to see. At this point in her career, Streisand certainly doesn't need the publicity photographs that young, aspiring stars crave so desperately. There was a time, however, when Barbra would roam the streets around Broadway, unknown, undisturbed. How far would her career have gone without the success of the FUNNY GIRL movie? Would she still be a New York City star only, belting the ballads in cabarets, longing for national exposure? Given the astounding range of her talent and voice, it is perhaps a bit ridiculous to even conceive of Barbra **not** becoming a superstar. **She** always knew she would.

And then there is that element behind the lens: the photographer. A photographic image is part of a universal language, but it brings with it the inherent sensibilities, prejudices, and style of the photographer. A photograph does not take itself; photographers train themselves to "see" for us. Photographers are artists as well, though they usually perform to the silent audience in the darkroom, or to the unknown public that sees their work and has no idea—and no desire to know—who has taken the picture. The photographer has an ego and a personality—he must be secure about his talent—like the celebrity he shoots. Yet the photographer is not congratulated for his performance, often harrassed, and disregarded while on assignment. The celebrity comes first. Barbra Streisand is capable of arousing violent reactions—by her public, and by those whose livelihood depends on transmitting her image (whatever she chooses it to be) to that public. Do the personalities of these stars affect the photographer as he works? Is he jealous—does he wish to take their place, have someone crave his image? How might this ambivalence—this ongoing love/hate relationship—show in a particular photograph; do, for example, photos of a well-liked star intentionally appear more flattering than those of another, less-liked celebrity? These questions, of course, can be answered by a yes or a no, and the answers vary, as you will read in the interviews, from one extreme to another. The ambivalent relationship between Barbra Streisand and these photographers does make the pictures—even the hurriedly-shot photo in the lobby—much more interesting to the viewer.

As I've mentioned, the photographers in this book often feel very strongly about Barbra—whether it's her style or look at a certain time, her voice, or their experiences shooting her. They have become, whether they are acquainted with her or not, **emotionally** involved with Barbra Streisand. Some of them expect—and dread—a confrontation. Some laugh at her stubbornness and mad dashes through hotel kitchens. Others are **hurt**, insulted, and degraded by Barbra's refusal to acknowledge their importance, their function, their livelihood, **them**. Perhaps this hurt only makes them more eager to succeed, to please not only Barbra but themselves. It is one of the intents of this book to provide more insight into the "why" and the "how" of a photograph. This can only be told by the photographers themselves.

The photographers interviewed in this book, from the world-renowned, elegant Cecil Beaton to the ubiquitous paparazzi Ron Galella, have had a wide range of experiences and encounters with Barbra Streisand—from the sublime to the ridiculous—and they are all remembered with a passion. Cecil Beaton thought Barbra had a "marvelous waif quality" and was a better photographic subject than Elizabeth Taylor. Yani Begakis remembered with happiness his backstage visit in Las Vegas when Barbra was surrounded by her show business friends. Bob Deutsch froze for hours on a street corner to get a shot of her during the filming of THE WAY WE WERE. Ron Galella missed a shot of Barbra with Canadian Prime Minister Pierre Trudeau and her manager never let him forget it. Tony Rizzo was attacked by Barbra's ex-husband Elliott Gould, took him to court, and watched as the judge asked Gould for an autograph (Rizzo won). Santiago Rodriguez tracked her down in the sub-basement of a parking garage and she was so amazed that he figured out where she'd be that she posed for him. Frank Teti was nearly trampled at the premiere of HELLO DOLLY! but managed to sneak in anyway.

During the course of the interviews, I decided to ask all the photographers similar questions: their background, where their pictures have appeared, the first and last times they've shot Barbra and how they got to meet her, their impressions of her style and appearance, how she changed as her career progressed (both physically and professionally), and any particularly noteworthy interactions they may have had. The purpose for this similarity was to see if the responses—despite the wide variance in photographic style and personality—would be similar. And in many cases, answers were identical, and interesting observations about Barbra Streisand began to be repeated: she prefers to be shot from her left side; she has an ongoing feud with the press; she hates to pose; she's difficult; she has the most interesting and beautiful face of any woman in the world; her voice is sublime; it's worth **anything** to be able to shoot her; she can—and will—do anything she wants. One other point agreed upon by all the photographers was their use of Nikon cameras (with the exception of Cecil Beaton, who was not asked that question).

Frank Teti originally planned for this book to be published around the time of Barbra Streisand's fortieth birthday on April 24, 1982, feeling that she had achieved such great success by that age and was a marvelous role model for women everywhere—with her beauty, talent, and unabating energy. A long-time Barbra-watcher, representative for photographers, and friend to most of the contributors in this book (with the exception of the late Cecil Beaton, who is, incidentally, his idol), Frank knew that Barbra's fans would appreciate a book that was not only a tribute to her talents but an unprecedented behind-the-scenes look by people who have followed her career since her first Broadway success as Miss Marmelstein in I CAN GET IT FOR YOU WHOLESALE. We decided on this format, hoping that the combination of photographs and interviews would add an intriguing edge to an already fascinating subject. In my research, I was amazed by the **passion** this woman has and continues to inspire—in photographers and fans alike. I was also struck by the shyness of most of the photographers I interviewed. Because they are so often seen as aggressive in pursuit of their subjects (although in most cases they are on specific assignments for popular magazines), we seem to have a preconceived notion of the personality of a photographer. Everyone I spoke to was amazed that we were interested in **their** point of view, and they were also most humble about their achievements and successes.

This book presents the multi-faceted Barbra Streisand. Through the lens, through many pairs of eyes, her career is traced from the streets of Brooklyn to the triumphs on stage and screen. As the kids, who hung out twenty years ago in Shubert Alley, armed only with seven-dollar Brownie Starflash cameras and a lot of love discovered, Barbra Streisand is indeed the greatest star.

—**KAREN MOLINE**
June 1982

NEAL PETERS COLLECTION

Michel Parenteau, a Streisand fan since 1965, sent her a print of his unusual birthday "card" displayed at Times Square in 1978. He did not expect a reply nor did he get one for many months, until he received an autographed, leather-bound script of THE MAIN EVENT (before the film was released) and an autographed photo.

Recording days, early sixties. MICHEL PARENTEAU COLLECTION

1963. BOB SCOTT COLLECTION

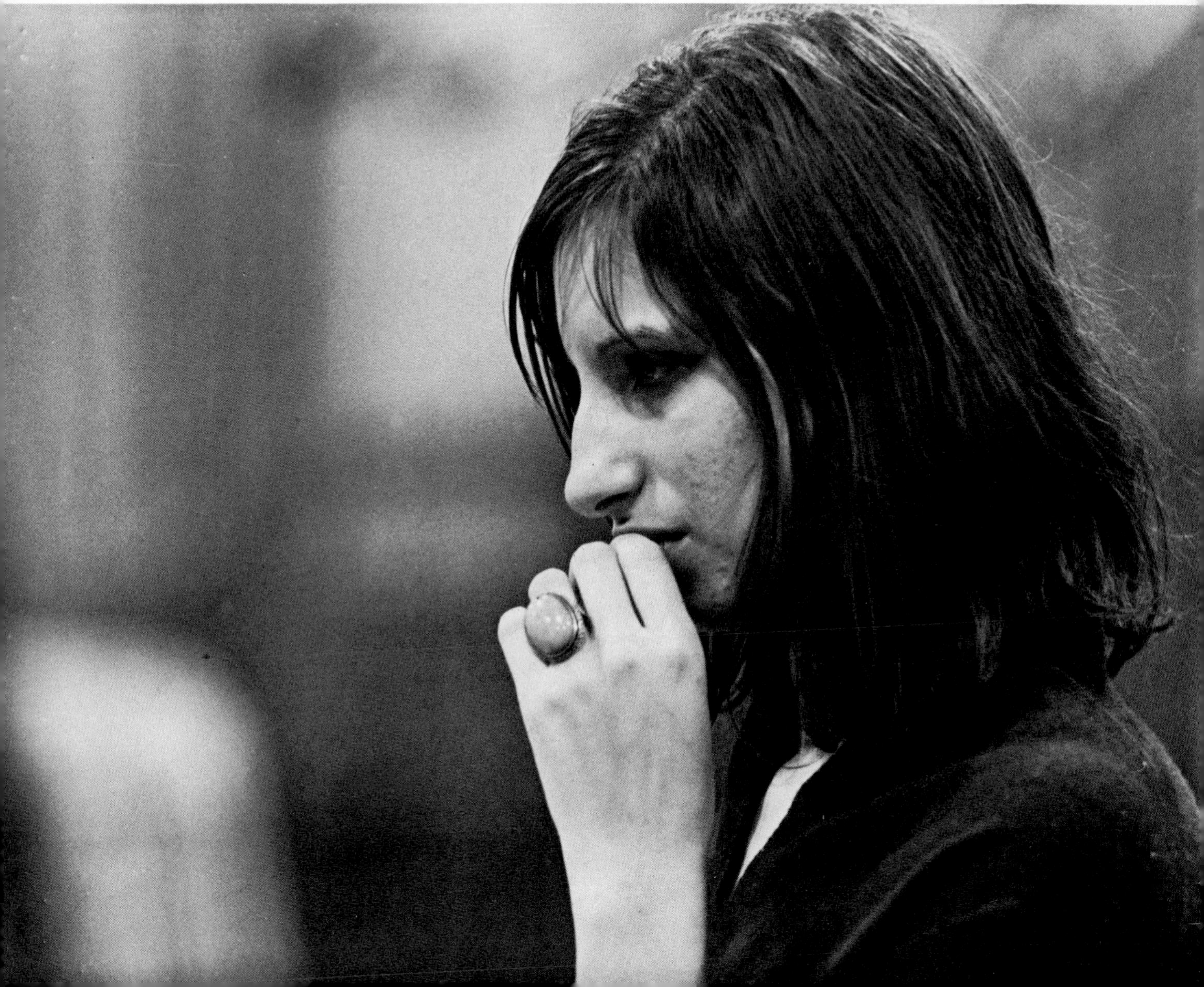

Fifteen years later—*Funny Lady*. MICHEL PARENTEAU COLLECTION

THE INTERVIEWS

All photographs in the following sections are by
the photographer interviewed unless otherwise credited.

"Unique and Very Talented"

BOB DEUTSCH

Born in June, 1945, Bob Deutsch became star-struck at the age of fourteen when his cousin Rona (an employee of CBS) got him tickets to THE GARRY MOORE SHOW. Enthralled, he bought his own tickets every week, and his career as a photographer began. He started with a cheap Starflash and soon graduated to 35mm. He continued to take pictures of the stars until he departed for the University of Georgia to study journalism. After returning to New York to work for a film company in 1970, he resumed photography of celebrities after-hours when he found money could be made from "fun work."

Bob Deutsch's photographs have appeared in TIME, NEWSWEEK, LIFE, LOOK, and many other publications. His shots from a session with Jacqueline Onassis resulted in the covers of McCALL'S, PARIS-MATCH, and BUNTE. His work has also appeared in THE SHAUN CASSIDY SCRAPBOOK, THE JOHN TRAVOLTA SCRAPBOOK, and a book on Diana Ross.

Mr. Deutsch is currently involved with soap operas and public relations.

KAREN MOLINE:
When did you first meet Barbra Streisand?

BOB DEUTSCH:
The first time I ever saw Barbra was on THE GARRY MOORE SHOW. I guess it was 1961. Frank Teti and Tony Rizzo, and I used to go every Friday. We became regulars because we loved Carol Burnett.

Where was the taping?
The Ed Sullivan Theater, which was then called Studio 50. Moore used a lot of Broadway talent, and Barbra was in I CAN GET IT FOR YOU WHOLESALE. We didn't know who she was except that she was in the play. And, I'll never forget this: I was sitting in the balcony with Tony Rizzo and suddenly he turned around and said, "Now Barbra Streisand will come out and sing." I turned to him and said, "Who?" She came out and started singing "Happy Days Are Here Again," wearing a raincoat. Tony said, "She's a really funny woman—watch, the song is gonna speed up and she's gonna do a strip." Of course, the song never sped up and she just sang and was incredible. From that moment on I just loved Barbra Streisand. When her first album came out, I immediately bought it.

How old were you then?
In 1961 I was sixteen. When I was sixteen, she was seventeen. Now she's forty and I'm thirty-six. I don't understand!

(OPPOSITE) Arriving at the stagedoor during the Broadway *Funny Girl,* 1964.

You were still in high school then. Did you have any idea what you wanted to do when you finished?

No. I still don't (laughs).

What began your career in photography?

When Frank, Tony, and I were going to THE GARRY MOORE SHOW every week, everybody was collecting autographs. That was the "thing." And we had met Carol Burnett—we were so in love with her—and gotten her autograph—so there was nothing else to do but take pictures of her. So we bought ourselves these little $7 Kodak Instamatics. Everytime we saw Carol Burnett with different people, instead of getting autographs, we'd take pictures. At the time it was very rare. There would be forty people lined up for autographs and just the three of us would have cameras.

Nobody else was taking pictures?

Very few.

How the world has changed! Everyone has a camera it seems.

Well, what's an autograph. It's just a name on a piece of paper. You look at it and it's nothing. But a picture—a star—I have pictures of myself with Carol Burnett.

Do you have pictures of yourself with Barbra Streisand?

No. Streisand to me has always been—I wouldn't say a goddess because that's real corny—but she's been untouchable. I've always been in fear of Barbra Streisand, and I still am to this day. She just really scares me. I can't deal with her on a personal basis. I've met her, I've photographed her, I can't say she's a friend, I can't say that she's even an acquaintance. I just can't deal with her. I come across as a fan, which I don't like, but I can't help it.

Has she sensed that—you being in awe of her—or do you try to hide it when you shoot her?

No, because the only times I've shot her is with other photographers around. Except in the very early days. It's too hard to deal with her— she is too big a star. She's **Barbra Streisand**.

Let's go back to Shubert Alley when Barbra was doing I CAN GET IT FOR YOU WHOLESALE. Did you wait for her after the shows?

Yes, but I didn't take very many pictures of her. I don't know why. I never knew she would become what she is. I just liked her as a singer. I shot a couple of pictures and then she left WHOLESALE, and did a guest spot on THE ED SULLIVAN SHOW. She had real long straight hair. A friend of mine and I went on a Saturday; that was when they rehearsed. And sure enough, she came in, and she was really friendly.

Do you remember what she said?

I said, "I really love your album," or something like that. And she said, "What would you like me to sing on my next album?" I said, " 'Over the Rainbow,'" and she said, "I can't do that—it's a Judy Garland song." Then I said, " 'Stormy Weather.' " And she said, "That's a Lena Horne song—I can't sing that either." I said, "Well, that's all my advice. I don't know what else to tell you!"

She never sang either of those on an album, did she?

No.

Did you see her in the play FUNNY GIRL?

Yes. When I went away to college, to the University of Georgia, I stopped doing photography. I went to study journalism. By then she had her second album out and I knew she'd be a **Big** star. I had gotten tickets to see the show before it opened, which was something I had never done before. I just loved it.

How did you get back into photography?

After four years of college and two years of working for a motion picture company in Georgia, doing documentaries, I came back to New York. I finally got a job and found I could make more money and had a better time taking pictures of movie stars.

What initially prompted you to pick up the camera?

The lack of money coming in on my job. I always wanted to work in something related to Hollywood. When I was thirteen years old I fell in love with TV—with this GARRY MOORE SHOW—and I always wanted

Walking in Shubert Alley, 1961.

(OPPOSITE) Durwood Kirby, Carol Burnett, Robert Goulet, Garry Moore, and Barbra on *The Garry Moore Show,* 1963.
MICHEL PARENTEAU COLLECTION

to be close to television. But when I went away to college I completely forgot about it. Never thought I would do it—really. I got a job selling equipment for a film company in New York, and I got to meet people who got me into big, celebrity parties. And as soon as I went to one party again, I went right back to the camera.

What system were you using?

I bought a Pentax, but it had one big disadvantage: the lenses didn't change easily. The company I worked for helped me get a Nikon real cheap. All I've ever used. So I went to these parties, nights, and I went to work in the morning and other nights worked in the darkroom, sold pictures, and it got to be a terrible burden. I was working seven days a week, making a lot of money. So I quit my job. It took me forever to make that break. It was such a scary thing.

When you had the entree to parties was it originally through friends?

One of the guys where I used to work was a cameraman for Hearst Metrotone News, which was like the newsreels in movie theaters. He gave me a police press card, which is the only thing which allows you to get behind the police press lines. The card was given to me illegally, and it's very hard to get—but he gave it to me anyway. So I'd read in the paper that so and so was having a party, and I'd call up and say that I was with Hearst News, and I [had] a press card. I'd get into everything. Anything I wanted to go to.

Did you build your own darkroom?

I had a little tiny apartment in the Village, and the darkroom was my kitchen.

Where did you start selling your pictures?

The first picture I ever sold was [of] George Harrison at the Bangladesh concert, for a fan magazine.

Do you remember how much you were earning per shot?

The fan magazines were paying something like $25 for black and white. I came in at the tail end of the fan magazines. They had been going strong since the '20s, '30s, and I started to sell to them in the early '70s. They were just about to start to die out. Not my fault, it just happened. Then along came PEOPLE magazine. Same gossip, a little cleaner. Then the STAR and the ENQUIRER came along. The fan magazines pay less now than in the early '70s, less than the '60s. You could get $1000 for a shooting then; now you're lucky if you get $150. So I had to change my markets. I can't spend five hours at Studio 54 on the odd chance I might get a shot. I do a lot of work now for public relations markets; I basically only work on assignment. I'm much happier. I don't like to go to parties anymore. I burned myself out about four or five years ago. (But I still go occasionally.)

It must have been a difficult decision to make because you had established yourself as a celebrity photographer.

I never liked the reputation of being a paparazzi. I'd much rather sit

24

home and watch TV. I would have to carry two cameras and two strobes and two lenses and twenty rolls of film with me, and I got to the point where I couldn't do it anymore.

What was the first shot you sold of Barbra?

I don't remember. It'll come to me later. I don't have many pictures of Barbra Streisand because she's my secret favorite.

What was your initial impression of her?

She was an ugly kid with a terrific voice. The first picture I ever took of her—my slide was stolen—is when she's coming from Erasmus High School, to go to work in WHOLESALE. Schoolbooks in her arms, her hair is stringy and long and falling all into her face. She was a real unattractive girl—with a terrific voice, just incredible. I never thought she would be a movie star; I only thought she had an incredible voice. In those days I liked Lena Horne and Doris Day. But when I heard Barbra Streisand sing, she moved me. Even when she did the musical FUNNY GIRL, she wasn't pretty. But she was unique.

That's the one word you'd use to describe her?

Unique and very talented. I have a videotape where she sings "I'm the Greatest Star"—and she's absolutely singing about herself.

What's your favorite expression about her?

"I'm the greatest star. I am by far." I'm sure she was saying to herself, "that's me, it's true, and you watch—I'm gonna be the biggest star in the world. . . ."

She certainly has the biggest inaccessible image.

That's what basically makes her such a shy person. I think she'd like to be more accessible. That's part of what makes Barbra Streisand that much more unique.

Don't you think that's due in part to her appearance?

No, I think it's Barbra. And as much as I hate her for being such a reclusive person, if she was more accessible, she wouldn't be Barbra Streisand. She can do anything.

What would you say is her most striking physical characteristic?

I wouldn't say her nose. I would say her **stare.** Eye contact. I've seen her look at me both in movies and in closeup. It freezes you.

Does she generally do that to photographers?

Generally she doesn't like to be photographed on the street. I spent a day shooting her on the set of THE WAY WE WERE. She did not want me on the set. I got in through my friend's police card. I knew they were shooting in front of the Plaza Hotel. I went to the director and said, "I'm Bob Deutsch, working for Hearst News (not true) and I was assigned to do the location today," and he said, "Well, let me check with Barbra." He came back and said, "OK, but don't get in her way." So I went on the other side of the barricade. Barbra was doing the scene with Redford, and I was standing right next to the camera. She was playing almost right to the camera, and she caught me and called the director over and said, "Get him away." I was interfering with her concentration. I can understand that—she was making a movie and she wanted to be left alone. I have this picture of her looking at me as if saying, "What the hell are you doing?" She had **every right** to think that, especially since I wasn't legitimately working that day. It was the only time I ever spent on a set with her.

Did you speak to her?

No. I spoke to some of the extras. One of them was a great Streisand fan. In one of the scenes he walks behind her—he doesn't have a speaking part—and he asked me to shoot a picture of them together. I did, and gave it to him, and I hope he's still thrilled with it.

Where did you sell those photographs?

Mostly the fan magazines. There was no great newsworthiness. I spent the whole time shooting Barbra, and this was just when Robert Redford was the Number One star.

Did you kick yourself?!

Not really. I was there because I loved Barbra Streisand. It was a thirty-degree day and I wouldn't have spent it if not for her. Streisand does her scene and goes back into her trailer where it's nice and warm. Me, I was standing out there for four or five hours. I wouldn't have spent five hours on the street for Robert Red-

The Way We Were, 1972.

30 A

ford. . . . When Barbra was shooting THE OWL AND THE PUSSYCAT, I was home from college for Christmas, and they were in New York. So I called up the film company saying I was a college student studying film and could they tell me where they were shooting. The girl said, "I can't tell you, but if you go to 358 East 58th Street, you may find them there." And they were there, Barbra and George Segal were doing the scene where she was out in the rain waiting for Segal to pick her up. They had hoses set up on the roof, making it rain. I just had a little camera; I didn't have any interchangeable lenses and couldn't do any close-ups. I was standing out here with my little camera, soaking wet, and the result was three prints where you won't recognize Barbra Streisand. It wasn't a great photographic job.

I loved her outfits in that movie. What do you think about her clothes and sense of style?

I always admired her for that because she could dress however she wanted to, and not only get away with it, but be really cool about it. I have copies of old LOOK magazines when she was married to Elliott Gould, and she was wearing all these weird clothes. But they look so terrific on her. Big long velvet dresses. That's all fashion is: if you really are admired by people, and you wear strange clothes, it's high fashion. I think Barbra dresses very well.

Did she always get away with this style, even when she wasn't as popular?

I think she became a real superstar right after FUNNY GIRL, and I don't think she's ever gone down from there.

Has she changed her style of dress? Is she still as eclectic as she was, or has she gone more Hollywood?

Now she's pretty much more standard. I just got a videotape of the 1975 Kennedy Center opening. She had really long blond hair—she dyed it—and she looks terrible. Real hideous. I can't believe that she actually dressed like that.

What do you think about her hair?

I liked it when she had real straight long hair in the beginning.

I don't think the curly hair is her, really, I think it's what Hollywood wants to have her look like.

I don't think that's true. In Barbra Streisand's case, she'll just do whatever she wants. I don't think it's Hollywood's idea at all. If she had any reason to shave off her hair and be bald, she'd do it. She doesn't make any excuses to Hollywood.

Has she ever?

Yes. When she originally signed to do FUNNY GIRL, she had a three-picture deal. When she went to London to do FUNNY GIRL on the stage—from what I've read—she desperately wanted to do it, but David Merrick told her that if she didn't stick out the two years on Broadway she wouldn't get the part in London. I don't know if it's true but I believe it. She stuck it out so she could go to London and then make the movie.

(OPPOSITE) Bob Deutsch's favorite photograph of Barbra.

Has there been any particular time in her life that she's been especially—or not—photogenic?

Looking back and thinking of that Kennedy opening, I think she looks hideous. Other than that, I like her. Some people say her curly hair makes her look like Little Orphan Annie. But I think she does what she can and she looks pretty good.

How much influence does Jon Peters have on her or her hair, at least?

I don't think anybody can influence Barbra Streisand. She's a really strong person. And you gotta believe that. What she wants to do, she does.

When you had the experience of watching her on the set, did she tend to take direction or give direction?

It was too hard to tell. I can tell you about the last time I saw her. About three years ago she received an award at the Pierre Hotel given by the Jewish organization, the B'nai B'rith. I was on assignment for NEWSWEEK and I went to shoot it. She was as nice as she could be.

Did she remember you at all?

No, I wish she did. I'd really like to have that kind of "Hi Barbra, Hi Bob" relationship. . . . There were about five or six other photographers there, but she was really charming and she posed. I took Michel Parenteau, who is a superfan, with me as my assistant. She had heard of him, because he had sent her a lot of letters and photos. He was very embarrassed, but he finally went up to her and introduced himself. I just had to say something so I said, "Welcome

back to New York. I wish you'd stay here and do some live concerts." She said, "Thank you very much." That was my whole conversation.

What's your favorite shot of her?

My favorite shot is at THE WAY WE WERE [set] when she's looking at me with those wicked eyes.

What is one of the things you remember the most when you were trying to shoot Barbra?

I can tell you what I regret the most. When she was doing WHOLESALE I really liked her. I also had just finished reading Lillian Roth's autobiography , I'LL CRY TOMORROW. Lillian was doing the show; she was the star. I went to get her autograph. She saw my autograph books and got real friendly because I was always hanging around Broadway. I'd go backstage and talk to her and go in her dressing room. She was nice. And I would be waiting and Barbra and Elliott Gould would come out and I'd say, "Hello, how are you." Now, looking back on it, I don't say I made the wrong choice, but I think that I could have had the same relationship with Barbra Streisand that I had with Lillian Roth.

But do you think you could have gotten close to her at that point?

Oh yes.

And so they accepted you as a friend of Lillian's.

I didn't want their pictures. I was waiting for Lillian. Even though I did like Barbra I didn't know I would love her. She was just a good singer.

With Jon Peters
at a B'nai B'rith
fundraiser.

Did you like the show?

I never saw I CAN GET IT FOR YOU WHOLESALE.

You never saw it!

At the time I didn't have anybody to go with. We were too busy going to TV shows, which were free. But I saw FUNNY GIRL many, many times. I saw the second half many more times than I saw the whole show. I would crash it—you can still do that— walk in at intermission. At the time, FUNNY GIRL was selling out. My most

embarrassing moment with Barbra Streisand had nothing to do with her. I had been to see FUNNY GIRL three or four times and I got my parents tickets and told them I'd meet them there and, in fact, that I'd see half the show. I met them at intermission and went to the Standing Room section. Out of the corner of my eye, as the lights were dimming, I saw the usher counting the people [still] standing. Obviously she counted one more than when she started. So she came around asking for ticket stubs. She got to me and I went through this whole act, because I didn't have a ticket stub. The lights went out and the overture started again, and I was creating such a stir, people were turning around. The head usher said, "If you were here for the first act, what was the closing scene of Act I?" So I said, "It was in the railroad station—'Don't Rain on My Parade.'" So they let me stay, and I was a nervous wreck.

How typical is Barbra compared to other celebrities you've shot?

I haven't shot her that many times that I can really say. Everytime I've shot her, as I've said, I'm really scared, because she's the consummate star. People say "star" in a bad way, but she's a star in every way—as far as talent goes. And when I meet somebody like that I get really scared, especially if I don't plan ahead. If I knew that half an hour from now I was going to Streisand's apartment, I could deal with it. But when things happen on the spur of the moment with her, I just can't. . . . If I'd see her walking in Central Park I think I'd just fall in the lake. It would be so unexpected.

Does she still have an apartment in New York?

I think she does, on Central Park West. In fact—to show you what kind of fan I am—everytime she comes to New York (I don't take my camera because I'd really be terrified to shoot her on the street) I'll walk down Central Park West, and I won't wait in front of the apartment but I'll always walk past to see if she'll come out,

see if she does any shopping at any of the neighborhood stores.

You go out of your way to go up there?

Yes, just on the off chance that I'd see her. I wouldn't do anything, I wouldn't bother her, I wouldn't say hello.

Does any other star make you feel that way?

I photographed Elizabeth Taylor when she was in THE LITTLE FOXES, in Florida, for NEWSWEEK. When it was over I went, "Oh my God, I just did Elizabeth Taylor," which I guess is not a very professional thing to do, but I didn't do it to her!

Would you react the same way if that happened with Barbra?

If I knew ahead of time, I'd be fine. I probably wouldn't be able to take her to dinner afterwards, though.

If you had a setup in advance, would you use particular lenses?

Because she's Barbra Streisand? No—she's no different from anybody else that way. I notice that she likes her left side photographed.

She instinctively turns her head if she knows she's going to be photographed?

Oh yes, ninety-nine percent of her pictures are always of her left side. I didn't really notice until in one of the lines in FUNNY GIRL, she said, "This is my best side." It's part of the movie, but I began to look at other shots and she's always photographed from that side. She obviously feels that's her better side. More power to her.

Sure, if she can get away with it.

She can because she's Barbra Streisand.

Do you think she can get away with just about anything?

So far. People mocked her a lot because she was doing the STAR IS BORN thing. It didn't do too well critically.

But it was immensely popular.

And this was her venture and she really believed in it. She made a lot of money from that. If you want to look at it from that perspective, then it was a very big success.

Did you hear the stories about her behavior during the production?

Oh yes. She was probably worse than other times because she had all her own money and reputation riding on it. Walter Matthau said he would never work with her again after HELLO DOLLY—and I'm sure that was all true. But she is a star in her own class. I admire strong people and she's very strong. And until she's proven wrong, there's no reason not to do it.

She was probably more nervous because A STAR IS BORN was her own project.

HELLO DOLLY was not her project; it was only her second movie. She had definite ideas. FUNNY GIRL is not Fanny Brice's story—it's Barbra Streisand's story. As much as I hate

that I really admire it. She gets away with it. And one thing she's always said is, "I pick the songs I sing." And that's Barbra Streisand. She deserves to get away with it—because that's what makes her Barbra Streisand.

Would you shoot her more often if you had the chance—despite how she intimidates you?

Definitely. I'd like to be able to work with her on a one to one basis. I'd like to have her come to this apartment and shoot her here. And I wouldn't feel terrible if she told me what to do. Because she has very definite ideas. I'm sure she has approval of all the pictures out (for record covers). Whatever she's doing, she's doing it right, because she's been a star—the Number One star since FUNNY GIRL opened, which was in 1967. I was in Central Park for her concert then—she had been filming in California and flew back.

What was the crowd like?

I got there with some friends at about two o'clock, and it was a good picnic. I brought a Manhattan phone book to sit on so I could see her and it worked. She came at about four and rehearsed the whole show, which was terrific. When she came back, and what stands out, was the crowd surging forward. In the afternoon, there were three of us on the blanket and by the time the show started there were twenty. It was really claustrophobic. She was not yet an international star; she was a New York star. The weather was terrific,

The concert in Central Park, June 1967 (LEFT), COURTESY CBS
and the famous "Don't Rain on My Parade" scene from *Funny Girl*.

she was terrific, but the crowds were real tight. But if she did it today I would spend eight hours waiting for her. I had gone to Newport, Rhode Island, in 1965 to see her in concert. It was on a football field—real flat—and I was extremely far away. I spent the entire concert looking at the back of the person in front of me. As I was leaving, the lady in front of me said, "$10 I paid to see a lousy pair of shoulders." But the sound was terrific. The best part of the evening was coming back on the ferry, someone had brought a little tape recorder with them and taped the whole concert, and we heard it all over again. Looking back it was worth it, but at the time it wasn't.

Do you see her as changing any career direction now?

I'm very curious about YENTL. I hope it's a big success for her sake. She's directing and producing and starring in it. She's the new Warren Beatty. A lot of people would like to see her flop because she's so high above anybody else.

It makes her seem more human?

Right. In a way I really hope she does well. I'm glad A STAR IS BORN was a big hit. People were saying every angle was done because it made her look the best. But I thought she was great because she sang, and she doesn't do live concerts anymore. If she did, it would be impossible to buy tickets—you'd have to beg for a ticket. The thing I dislike about her now is that she doesn't sing live anymore. Everybody wants to hear her sing.

"Very Gifted"

SANTIAGO RODRIGUEZ

Raised in Spanish Harlem, Santiago Rodriguez currently is based in Los Angeles. His work has appeared in many publications, including TIME, NEWSWEEK, LOOK, PEOPLE, PHOTOPLAY, and various tabloids. His pictures of Presidents Kennedy and Reagan have appeared in news magazines around the world, but his most famous cover shot was of Ann-Margret—it appeared on the front cover of PHOTOPLAY, OGGI in Italy, and PARIS-MATCH. Mr. Rodriguez's favorite show business subjects are Annette, Ann-Margret, Diana Ross, Leslie Uggams, and Joey Heatherton.

Santiago Rodriguez is also involved in the recording industry in Los Angeles, and he has been an avid record and tape collector for over twenty years.

KAREN MOLINE:
What sort of photography do you do?

SANTIAGO RODRIGUEZ:

I do the same kind of photography that Frank [Teti] and Tony [Rizzo] do—that's how we all met. When we lived in New York, Frank was the one who started me doing it professionally. One day he just decided he was going to open an agency, and he wanted to know if we'd shoot for him. And I said yes. That was about twelve years ago. Streisand was one of the people I shot. She was one of the more difficult ones. I started shooting everybody.

When did you leave New York to move to California?

I left in April of 1965. I couldn't take the cold anymore and I left. It was the wisest move I ever made.

And you've been in Los Angeles ever since.

Ever since. I was eighteen when I left [New York].

Where is most of your photography published?

Movie magazines. I refer to them as "film periodicals" (laughs).

When did you first shoot Barbra?

The first time was walking down Shubert Alley. I already knew that she was in the show I CAN GET IT FOR YOU WHOLESALE, but I hadn't seen it. She passed me down the street, and I followed her and I asked if I could get

Rodriguez's
favorite portrait
of Barbra.

a picture. She seemed quite reluctant. She said, "You don't want my picture," and I said, "Yes, I do. I saw your show and I thought you were great," which wasn't true; I hadn't seen her. And she finally said, "Oh, OK," and I got a reasonably good picture. That was the first encounter. So one thing I will always say for her: she didn't become nasty overnight. She was always totally indifferent to being photographed. It isn't like it happened because she got a temper—she **never** liked doing it. Only early in her career, you could sort of like talk her into it. You could say, "Oh, come on, I think your album was terrific," and then she'd say, "Oh, well, OK." But now, well, it's a whole other story.

When was the last time you shot her?

The last time I shot her I happened to have been alone. It was at the opening of THE WAY WE WERE at Century City, which was a circus, because it was a premiere. I had the feeling that she wasn't going to come out of the theater the way she went in. At the Century City complex, they have underground parking. So I just happened to write down the license plate number of the car she arrived in, and about a half-hour before the show was over, I went down the elevator path to see if the car might be waiting by one of the lower levels near an elevator. I spotted it about five levels down. And I waited. Eventually she came out, and I asked if I could get a couple of pictures. She was so flabbergasted at my having figured it out. She said, "Well, if you were smart enough to figure out that

His first shot of Barbra, 1962.

40

I'd be sneaking out this way, why not." She actually threw me a bone, in fact; she stood there and let me take about four or five pictures. And that was it. That was the last time I saw her.

Aren't you clever!

It will never happen again! I have had other episodes with her. Once, I don't remember what the circumstances were, I again happened to have been alone, and she was with a group of people. So I waited until she came out of wherever she was, the hotel lobby, to wait for her car. I asked her if I could get a picture. She thought for a minute, and said, "Well, just one." She pointed at me and repeated, "Just one." And I took it and the flash didn't go off. She got hys-

terical, I got hysterical. I got frantic! There she was, standing, waiting . . . so I started shaking my camera and screaming, "Wait a minute! Wait a minute! Let's take a remake. You're in the movies, let's do a remake." So she allowed me the courtesy of taking one more shot. And the flash went off.

It came out OK?

It came out fine.

What was she wearing?

I don't know—some fur coat. Nothing spectacular. Because it wasn't at a public function or anything, and I was there for something else and just happened to spot her in the lobby. The picture was no great photographic feat. It was just the idea that there she was, willing, and my camera doesn't function. Very frustrating.

What was your very first impression of her—did you think she was going to be a star?

It's kind of hard. I didn't really think of it at the time. Because I learned, when I first started taking pictures and getting involved with celebrities and films, that it doesn't really deal with your appearance. If you've got it, you've got it. When I saw her, I said to myself—I wondered—what it was she did in the show that she was getting these wonderful reviews for. Then when I heard her sing, I thought, well, that's it. It doesn't matter what she looks like, with a voice like this.

It's interesting you feel that way, since you're a photographer and deal with the visual aspect of celebrities.

I've **never** dealt with appearances. I just remembered that she came out past me and I thought: Oh, that's the girl in the show. As I followed her, getting my camera out, it didn't run through my mind what she looked like. I kept thinking: well, I better get her picture because she's gotten all these great reviews; she's gonna be hot stuff. One other time I spotted her walking down Sixth Avenue. She went into a restaurant by Radio City Music Hall, and that was one of the two times I saw her with Elliott Gould. Just before they went in the door, I got one quick shot of them. They were both fairly nice about it. Another time I saw them going into the Paramount Theater on Times Square for a midnight show. She was still in WHOLESALE, and going out at midnight for someone in the theater wasn't unusual. I got one or two pictures before she went through the door. When she was in the theater, you could see her wandering around going to and from work just like everybody else. You didn't really think about it. You'd just say, "Oh, there's Barbra Streisand again."

Didn't her mother chaperone her around?

I think she did. I never paid much attention to her. And I was very careful to keep relatives out of pictures if I could possibly help it. I could have seen her mother, but if I did, I didn't take any note of it.

What stands out about Barbra physically?

After looking at a couple of my pictures, I kept thinking that she doesn't look like your typical Broad-

(OPPOSITE) After the Tony Awards, 1963.

way ingenue. This is before I got to her singing style. I thought, well, she's obviously got something I don't see, if she's getting those kind of notices. Since I wasn't into her singing, I thought to myself that I couldn't deal with her since her "something" wasn't visible to me yet.

How do you think she's changed over the years in terms of her appearance or how she projects herself?

The only thing that I think has changed constantly about her appearance has been her hair. I get the impression that she tries to follow the trends that happen to be around at the time.

You don't feel she's interested in setting the trend?

No. If it happens to look good on her, she'll keep a style. And if they don't happen to look good on her, she gets rid of them. You know, her long straight look, and that frizzy look, and now that kind of curly-type look.

Performing at the Friar's Club tribute to her, May 16, 1969.

Is there any style that you particularly like?

I like the beginning style, both vocally and appearance-wise. I like her choice of material early [in her career], her singing style early, and her appearance early; everything say up to and including around FUNNY GIRL. She was just wonderful in that part.

Has she gotten more Hollywood now?

Yes, but for music, she manages to stay ahead of everybody else who might make a record along with what might happen to be fashionable at the time. But for some reason hers work. She seems to put more work into it because she's followed every conceivable style around, and always manages to come up with a hit somewhere along the way. I don't know how she does it.

She's psychic.

I did prefer her earlier style because I like that kind of music better.

Did you ever notice her fingernails?

Yes. The first time I spotted them was when she was fumbling with her bag when she was posing for me. And I remember thinking, "What nails!" I asked myself if they were hers or part of the character she was playing in the show. Later I realized it was part of her style.

How would you rate her—considering all the celebrities you've shot—as being more difficult, less difficult, or just like any other star?

I would definitely rate her as more difficult. I'm sure it's just her manner. She doesn't want to be bothered, and with the kind of talent she has, she can get away with it. Of course, I've had my one or two instances where I managed to get a couple of shots on my own, but generally, as a rule, she's definitely in the more difficult category. Or **most** difficult (laughs).

Partly because she puts herself in few social situations where she can be photographed.

And consequently, when she does go out, it's so unusual that everybody wants to get their pictures. They may not see her again for months.

In a sense she's a prisoner of her own celebrity. She doesn't go out often, so when she does, she knows she's going to be deluged. Don't you think that if she found a more compromising attitude it might be easier for everybody, including herself?

Oh yes. Even if she didn't go out often, if, when she did, she'd stand there and let the photographers get so many pictures that the market would be flooded, then there would be so little demand, and she would be just like everybody else. But because she makes it very difficult when she does go out, you have to scramble. I've been doing this so long, I go from one season to another where you go out to a function and there's one person—that season—who is the most photographed person. And you cannot get enough pictures. And then a year from then, no one cares; you can't give away the pictures. But with Streisand, there always seems to be a genuine demand. She always manages to stay on top because of her films and records, and since she doesn't go out often, people want pictures when she does. She won't give it a chance—in and out the kitchen doors.

Were you at the infamous screening of WILLY WONKA AND THE CHOCOLATE FACTORY when she came out with Jason?

Oh yes. It was on a Sunday afternoon, a nice day, and we thought, well there'll be a small turnout, we'll spend an hour and get out of there. But it was a zoo. Big turnout, lots of celebrities. Ali McGraw, Annette Funicello, et cetera. We were all standing around shooting, and out of the blue, in she walks, didn't even run—walks—with Jason. And we just freaked out. Naturally when she sat inside, she didn't sit at the edge; she sat in the middle, making it very difficult to get any decent pictures. People were screaming and carrying on. We had to wait till she came out. She

came up once to go to the restroom with Jason—he was small at the time so she went to the ladies' room with him—and then this strange woman, out of the blue, came out. She started yelling at us, "Why don't you people leave her alone!"

Barbra must have spoken to her in the ladies' room.

Funny how nobody paid her any attention anyway. But Barbra did go out the back, and there are stairs, and it was just a mess. If you had a decent position, you could get something, and if you didn't, well, then you were out of luck.

Were you lucky?

I don't know. A couple of black and whites. She didn't make it easy on us. Everybody had to scramble for what they got. There's my point again. She **had** to go out that way; she knew we were going to be out there; if she had just stood there for five minutes, and let everybody shoot, then at least the pictures that they did get would have been flattering. Instead you get pictures of her running, and looking down and looking around. So if she's going to get shot anyway, if she would stand there, she would at least get a shot where she doesn't have her mouth open. I really don't think she takes that into consideration. I think her main thing is: **They** won't get anything. If she's not going to give us anything, and we have to really work for one shot, then it's not going to be as flattering than if she posed. What to do (laughs)!

With Jason at the infamous premiere of *Willy Wonka* in 1971.

She has to have absolute control over all her shots.

I'm sure that if she had her way, and she let us stand there and take pictures, she would want to see **every** shot in exchange for standing there. And then she'd say, "OK, you can have these two back, the other three I'm keeping." If she could arrange that, she would. Then everybody would get their pictures. But she can't control the elements away from her sets. On a set she sees everything; outside, in public, she can't do that. So she thinks, if I can't control it, you're not gonna get **any**.

Do you think that as a person and in her private life she's as difficult as she is in her public life?

Professionally, probably yes. But I'm sure that her personal relationships with friends and lovers are very pleasant. Professionally, it's got to be her way. And she seems to have a natural instinct for picking out what's best as far as her talent is concerned. Time after time she's proven herself right. How can you argue with that track record?

You can't. She's a superstar.

So she **will** get it her way, one way or another. She'll prove them right; she'll prove them wrong everytime.

You can't argue with it. That's why she's Number One.

And she'll keep being Number One, and people will just have to go along with it. That's the way it's gonna be.

Have you ever shot any specific events? Do you go to the awards ceremonies in Hollywood?

I don't go to the Oscars. I stopped going because there's so much competition, and there are so many people that I see at every other event—I got tired of going! I go to things like the Directors' Guild and the Golden Globes. She's been to a couple of those. Those situations are usually a different story. While she may go in through a back door and come out a back door, if she wins she knows that there is an expected situation between a winner and photographers. And I'm always amused, when I see somebody who doesn't like doing it, in a situation they can't get out of. And I think to myself, well, good for you, here you are, trapped (laughs).

Do you get different shots then; does Barbra look differently or does she put on a face?

No, she doesn't look any different. And the pictures are all more or less the same, you know. You stand against a given background, holding whatever award, with or without whoever presented it to you. She's obligated to do it; if she had her way, she wouldn't be there. But I do notice that she doesn't stay long. Usually there are so many photographers that the setup is made so that when the person comes back, there are three different spots for them to stand. I saw Barbra at one Grammy Awards where she went through the room in six seconds. I only got the pictures because I was standing on a chair. She stood at the first position for four seconds, and left the room. I've never seen anything so fast in my life. Everybody was complaining. But she can't say she didn't go! She did go—she just didn't stay very long. But I think four seconds is a record. I focused, got four frames and suddenly she's out of the room.

Did you sell those photos?

Yes, but there was nothing unusual about them. She had a nice look to her, but she was at a public event and not that many pictures were taken. She might as well not have come back at all for what she allowed us to take. Very funny. I thought it was funny because I got one or two shots. It was funny to watch everybody react; they got **nothing.** Of course if I hadn't gotten anything I wouldn't have thought it was so funny!

So she ranks among your most unco-operative subjects.

Yes, but there again, with that kind of talent, she gets away with it.

Have you ever noticed any specific moods when you've seen her?

It's always the same. I'll see her come out of a function, and the mood will immediately get tense if she sees that we have spotted her, we are coming towards her. She may walk out with a group of people, talking and smiling, but the minute she sees that she's about to be pounced upon, it changes altogether. The conversation stops, and she's headed right for the door, and for the car. And God forbid that car should not be there.

I've seen situations where the car has not been there.

What has she done?

She stands there looking down at the ground, or looking at the shoulder of her escort, making it difficult to get anything. Depending on the escort, the reaction is funny. When she first started dating Jon Peters, she went to a big sporting event. Everybody in town was there and **everybody** had to wait for their cars. Even Elizabeth Taylor. Well, when Barbra came out—it was one of the first times she was out with Jon in public—she started pulling this routine, and Jon said to her, "Why don't you just stand there and let them get a few pictures and they'll leave you alone?" She was **furious.**

You actually heard him say that?

I heard it. She was being defied, but of course that attitude didn't last for long. She rubbed off on him real fast. After a while he would be the one pulling her into and out of the cars. But that was the first time and he was probably very amused by it. She was literally surrounded, because she couldn't go anywhere, and if she had stood there and looked straight out, even without changing the expression of her face, everybody would have gotten their pictures. Jon Peters thought the whole thing was a big joke. The event—an indoor boxing match at the Beverly Hilton—was listed in the papers so every photographer in town was there. But even Elizabeth Taylor let us get what we wanted. Not Barbra!

With Peter Bogdanovich at the Director's Guild Awards, Beverly Hilton Hotel.

Have you had any other contact with men in her life besides Jon?

One time she went with Peter Bogdanovich to the Director's Awards. That's usually a light turn-out. This ceremony is very nice for photographers: not only do they invite us to cover, but they invite us to stay and have dinner. Well, about half an hour before it was going to start, you figure everyone has already arrived, so you go in and sit down. For some odd reason I didn't go in; I was standing in the lobby talking to my friends. And Barbra got out of a car not five feet from me, with Peter Bogdanovich. I couldn't believe my luck, so I started shooting away. In between the time she walked into the lobby, checked in at the door, and walked through, I must have gotten a good fifteen to twenty pictures. And then, of course, when she got to her table she was surrounded. It didn't take long for her to have her people chase everybody away. She was holding a program up to her face—those kinds of shots. As she left it was the usual running shot.

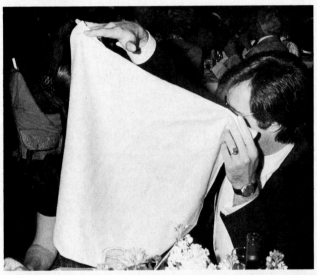

Does it bother you when this happens?

Yes it does. It's very irritating because it's not necessary. You expect it from her. You would be disappointed if she stood there and posed! It's so unnecessary because everybody else does it; the ones who don't like doing it understand that it's part of the game. They stand there, they do it for five minutes, and it's over with.

Can she possibly get any pleasure out of being so difficult? I guess

she's got too much pride to capitulate.

Well, I don't know if she gets any pleasure out of it. I guess she feels, well, they're going to start in on me, I'll just start in on them back. That's the only thing I can think of. Maybe she never sat down to realize that if the market was flooded, no one would care. Presley was the same way. **He** wasn't that difficult, but the people around him made it so difficult that there were no pictures in circulation. So when you got a couple you were able to place them.

Do you have a favorite shot [of Barbra]?

One, at a Golden Globes, one of the early ones. She and Clint Eastwood had been named world film favorites that year. She had her long, stringy hair at that time, and a pillbox hat.

What's a particular word or expression to describe her?

A flattering term or a non-flattering term?

Both.

Well, a non-flattering term—it's the same old word from before: **Difficult.** Which I'm sure everybody applies to her. Until she actually stops working, that word's always going to apply. It'll be her way because she's right, and that's the way it's going to be. But the flattering term, I would say, [is] **very gifted**. She's got something that no one else has.

Do you have a favorite movie [of Barbra's]?

Probably FUNNY GIRL, because it was the first one on the screen, and I had seen the play. For people who had only seen her on television and had never heard her closeup, like the way you would see her on a giant screen, here was a face destined to become huge. And she wasn't someone who looked like Raquel Welch or Ann-Margret. She had a unique look all her own. And it was going to defy and break all the rules—and come out on top. And that's exactly what she did. That's all I thought of when I saw FUNNY GIRL. I was already familiar with her talent, I had seen her on [TV] specials, had all her records, seen her on stage, but that movie indicated to me that the people not already familiar with her were not going to be ready for this. One of the early shows I saw her on was THE GARRY MOORE SHOW, when she and Robert Goulet were guests. They rode out on a little golf cart. She was very, very young and I said to myself, what is this woman doing on a cart with Robert Goulet? Of course, when she started singing it was totally unimportant.

It wasn't important what she was doing or what she looked like?

When she opened her mouth and started singing, you realized that it didn't matter. Her appearance went right out the window.

You do forget what she looks like when she's singing.

That's true. That's what I thought when FUNNY GIRL came out, because on the album, she just had that one still shot. You can't really see a person animated from a still. I knew FUNNY GIRL was going to bring her tremendous attention.

She's very ambitious to be doing a project like YENTL.

She has taken chances like that before—like the music changes from album to album. She tries to do the same thing with movies but she seems to be more successful with records. You can't win 'em all! She still dominates the record field in one form or another.

Yes, but A STAR IS BORN was not exactly a critical success, yet it made millions and she was the one who put her money into it.

Exactly.

If you're going to measure success in how much money you make, she certainly never has lost anything.

She hasn't. Then again, she had it her way, and they all defied her, and she came out winning, and she had the last laugh. So the next time they won't be so quick to argue with her or they'll be fired.

There's been very little comment about YENTL, and she's directing, producing, and starring.

Doing the whole thing? Here we go again. Well, she's got her following, and on her following alone she can't miss. The kind of reviews a picture gets don't matter, because people will go anyway. If the movie's a real turkey, she sings a few songs, and the soundtrack will sell millions.

She always has wanted to be seen as an actress, not just a singer, but she doesn't seem to realize that her following doesn't want to see her as much that way.

No, they want to hear her sing, no matter what it is. This way she gets to do a little bit of everything. She will always be singing.

Have you ever done any studio shots with her?

No. I would wonder how to approach a situation like that. With a lot of apprehension—really. I know what I'm doing photographically, but I would go there fully expecting to be told "You stand there."

That's what I was going to say. She'd tell you exactly what to do.

And, of course, I would do it. Because I wouldn't care. If I had an assignment and I were going to be paid, I would do it her way just to keep her quiet. But I wouldn't miss an opportunity to see that kind of direction. Something I've heard so much about. I wouldn't miss the opportunity to have her tell me, "OK, the light is going to be coming from my left, therefore you shoot it three feet from my right and not two, and not four, but three." I would do it, and it would be something I'd always remember.

Does she prefer to be shot from her left side?

I think so. She goes on and on about the lights not being hot enough or not bright enough or something like that. I'm always amused by that reaction.

Do the other photographers who've shot her in sessions talk about her?

Yes—always very disparagingly. I'll ask them how it went, and they might say something like, "How do you think it went!" instead of, "Oh, it went very well." I want to say to them, "What did you expect when you went there?" But they always fully expect that under those circumstances it's going to be different. I would go there fully expecting a session where I do exactly as I'm told. I guess these people went there thinking that since it's a setup, and a private thing, they're going to be able to tell her what they want done. That's not the way it works in her case. Maybe under normal circumstances, but not in her case.

Have you ever shot her on movie sets?

No. They're always outdoorsy-type things, and she really can't control people in crowds. If a person was standing with a long lens, out of range where they're told not to stand, she couldn't do a thing about it. I know that would irritate her no end.

She has to know that's going to happen.

She's out of luck. But that's why, instead, she has full control. I'll tell you a story that someone told me about Barbra and the Foreign Press Association. When somebody comes out here to do a film, the studio arranges a luncheon with the lead and the members of the Hollywood Foreign Press. After a lunch and a question and answer period, each

member has their photograph taken with the star. Well, apparently Barbra was counting frames that the photographers were taking, and she demanded all the rolls of film back and no one ever got any of those pictures. She saw how many members there were, knew exactly how many rolls of film would cover her, and got them back. I thought that was hilarious. They were furious, but I wasn't surprised.

They never appeared in print?

They never appeared. And they were just pictures that, if you had an interview, you would print it later when you ran a column. That's all the pictures were for. But she didn't care. She counted heads, figured out how many to a roll, and the number of rolls of film back. Never seen again.

That seems a bit paranoid.

I look at it as funny because I don't like to think of anybody as so far gone. I don't know, maybe she is.

We'll never know.

I'm sure there are a lot of stories like that that we will never ever know. But the ones I do know, I can enjoy.

How many stories can you hear? It's the same thing over and over.

Usually a bit on the negative side. But then as you follow her and her style through members of the press, after awhile, it almost appears to be normal behavior for her. . . . That time at the parking lot, when I had her alone, she just said to me, "Well if you were smart enough to figure this out, you can take a few." But I was by myself. Normally what I would have said

Hello Dolly. BOB SCOTT COLLECTION

was, "Can I just take one or two quick frames?" Yet at the next party, she didn't go in the front and she came out through the kitchen. She changed once and went back to her old habits. You never really know what you're going to get. When she is nice, you always remember, because you don't get it that often.

Did you ever have an embarrassing experience with her?

Only the one time she told me I could get a picture and the flash didn't go off. And the most frustrating. There she is saying yes, and my camera is saying no. And then after all that, nobody wanted it! There was nothing different about the picture, she was just standing, looking into the camera, smiling. You could have gotten it free from the studio. But you'd think that after all that work . . . .

Of all your experiences with her, which one do you remember the most?

The one in the parking lot and the one with the flash. Because I was alone each time, and there was cooperation on her part. Both instances are very, very rare; you don't usually get her alone or cooperating. I had a little bit of an exclusive and I'll always remember those. It's like getting into an elevator with her. What do you think those chances are?

She probably doesn't take elevators.

That's right (laughs)! She goes up to the roof and then she's lowered down on a crane.

55

Cecil Beaton, on Streisand

BY GEORGE HADDAD-GARCIA

FRANK TETI

SIR CECIL BEATON

who died in 1980, was known worldwide as one of the most elegant and talented, to say nothing of charming, designers of sets and costumes in show business. Multi-faceted, he was also renowned for his skills as a photographer and painter. He won three Academy Awards: two for the set and costume designs of MY FAIR LADY, and one for his costumes in GIGI. Once engaged to Greta Garbo, an intimate of the Royal Family in England, friend to many in the business over the long span of his career, Sir Cecil was beloved and revered in the industry for his talent and style.

ABOUT
GEORGE HADDAD-GARCIA

George Haddad-Garcia is a San Mateo, California-based journalist and actor. A communicator, he is most interested in media and travel. He speaks six languages and has traveled in thirty-six countries. His first American book is THE FILMS OF JANE FONDA, published in 1981. Part-English, Jewish, and Mexican, he is a Zen Buddhist, and is now concentrating on writing screenplays in English and acting in any tongue.

George Haddad-Garcia arranged to interview the late Sir Cecil Beaton through friends of his late grandfather, who was the ambassador from Mexico to England after World War II. He met with Sir Cecil in 1979, first in Paris and then at Beaton's home in Salisbury, England. Beaton was semi-retired at that time.

Sir Cecil arriving with Lee Radziwill at the premiere of *Coco* (OPPOSITE), and with Barbra in her dressing room during the filming of *On A Clear Day* (ABOVE).

MICHEL PARENTEAU

In Hollywood, the late Sir Cecil Beaton was known as the man who won two Academy Awards for MY FAIR LADY, while legendary director George Cukor won a solitary Oscar for directing the musical. (Beaton won for his sets and costume designs.) The Englishman was an accomplished theatrical designer, writer, wit, and photographer. He remains best known for his wide body of photography—of Edwardian ladies in London, of Hollywood stars during the cinema's golden age, of Britain's royal family, and for covering World War II with his far-ranging camera.

Perhaps his single greatest achievement was the look of MY FAIR LADY, already considered a classic on Broadway in the '50s and Hollywood in the '60s. However, Beaton's other classic work won him an Academy Award for GIGI in costume design, and raves for similar work in ON A CLEAR DAY YOU CAN SEE FOREVER, his last major assignment. For Barbra Streisand's Brighton and other Regency period scenes, he created some of his most lavish wardrobe conceptions. The film was a relative failure at the box office, but the picture within a picture won high praise and gave a glorious hint of what might have been achieved, had Beaton and Streisand collaborated on an English or Continental picture of their own.

NEWSWEEK, while decrying the film in general, applauded the combination of two such individual trend-setters: "She's a thoroughbred clotheshorse for Cecil Beaton's costumes."

The two got on famously, according to all reports. Barbra was in awe of the man's visual sense, of the drama and style he had been manifesting in several fields since his youth. For his part, Sir Cecil found that "Barbra is one of two kinds of superstars. The two types are: the coolly detached and the fanatically involved. Barbra was the latter, during our collaboration in ON A CLEAR DAY YOU CAN SEE FOREVER.

"The former type of superstar is typified by Audrey Hepburn, with whom I collaborated in MY FAIR LADY. Both women are very different, yet they're both regal, and that came through in the clothes I designed for them. Audrey cared about quality, too, but wasn't mesmerized by movies. Barbra and I talked our way into everything, and I trusted her judgment, something I seldom do with any actor, especially a relative neophyte (CLEAR DAY was only the third

Streisand movie). She obviously thought everything out; I've never, to this day, met anyone so young who had such an awareness and knowledge of herself."

He recalled that both Hepburn's and Streisand's wardrobes included before-and-after outfits. "Melinda (Streisand's character) came from lower-class origins and was dressed in a rather grubby, unflattering manner, much as Eliza Doolittle during her Covent Garden days. Both women were marvelous at conveying this earthiness, and seemed to relish the chance to wear rags and carry on like craven guttersnipes," he stated with amusement. "But as grand ladies, dressed to the hilt, they were truly in their element, aware that everything had been building up to that moment—neither had a lack of confidence in their ability to act regal and look monumental, despite their widely varying types and images. Audrey had a best-dressed, Givenchy-type of image, while Barbra was better known for her youthfulness, even her zany quality. Of any actress I've ever worked with, I believe she had the widest range as a performer. At the time, she was only in musicals, but I'd be very much surprised if she isn't given the opportunity, in future, to prove herself an accomplished dramatic actress of style and variety."

Observers claimed that the leading lady got on better with the genteel Englishman than most of her other co-workers. A gentleman to the bone, Sir Cecil admitted to treating "Miss Streisand" more like a lady with intelligence than a box-office

(OPPOSITE) Photograph and clothing design by Beaton, 1969.

freak—something the twenty-seven-year-old wasn't that used to. He had nothing but praise for her work in ON A CLEAR DAY, but allowed that he hadn't seen her subsequent films and was in no position "to give her all-around endorsements."

But he offered, in 1979, "I recall one of the reviewers found the Streisand performance as an English aristocrat reminiscent of vintage Joan Greenwood. I enjoyed reading that, because both women display a quality of cunning refinement. Barbra did an English accent to perfection; perhaps in an earlier life she was a landed lady with titles and royal lovers. It is a pity Barbra doesn't do more period material. She is an ideal mannequin and a compelling actress in elegant period costumes. Her face is a painting from several historical eras. Barbra as an Englishwoman, an Egyptian, or a Ming empress would be unforgettable.

"The public sees her as very contemporary, but I think her soul is old-fashioned, and in all honesty, she was far more likeable, more at ease, in the old English sequences of the picture than as the neurotic college student in those dreadful mini-skirt creations!"

Rumors of Streisand's "feuds" with directors, leading men, and other associates are practically legendary, if usually disproven, but Beaton insists, "We didn't quarrel. We got on beautifully. Both our reputations were on the line. She had had two previous musicals; this one had to be different, and I had done things like GIGI and MY FAIR LADY, so how could I top myself? We topped ourselves visually." This time out, Beaton didn't have to design any sets. Instead, George IV's Royal Pavilion at Brighton was finally opened by the authorities to location shooting.

The esthetic highlight of ON A CLEAR DAY YOU CAN SEE FOREVER was a Brighton banquet sequence for which Beaton designed Barbra's startling white and silver ensemble. Not only a flowing, empire-cut gown, but a beehive headdress which hid her hair, and accentuated her "historical features." Not a few Streisand fans feel that in this scene, their idol was at her most beautiful, her most sensuous, and simultaneously her most refined, from all the scenes in all her movies.

Sir Cecil said of that scene, "It was inspired—and both our ideas, really—to wrap the Streisand features in a glorious white turban, to further accent her strong features. At the same time, she was totally feminine, beguiling, shamelessly sexual. In my designs, her look was soft, almost maternal, but very beautiful, as in a Raphael painting. I tried to stress the lushness of the fabrics, the intricate designs and motifs, in short, the physical if not spiritual splendor of the period we were dealing with. On a less gifted actress and model, on almost any American actress I can think of, this would have been wasted and somewhat ludicrous. Barbra has a less monotonously American-type [look] than most actresses of her nationality," he stated matter of factly.

Much of their collaboration occurred prior to the actual filming, when clothes and hair concepts were

60

presented and then finalized. "She said yes easily, and she said no easily—not to exercise a star's prerogative, but to discard anything she felt wasn't in her range or in keeping with her character in the picture." Like many celebrities who are well acquainted with and admiring of each other's style, Beaton and Barbra did not become chums, nor kept in regular touch upon completing their mutual assignments. Beaton explained, "She was charming to work with, almost literally. Like a hypnotist. We were not terribly close, and I didn't want a closeness that would alter my feeling of her as a self-willed creation. I had that in mind when I designed; I tried to forget the Streisand image, whatever that was. I understand there were unfavorable remarks that the picture itself was weighted down with the English settings and costumes, but I confess I found them the best part of the picture, apart from Barbra's compelling presence.

"Pleasing her was very difficult, but it pleased me, inwardly, because I myself am extremely hard to please. I think each of us is ever aware of the name we've been given and, more importantly, what we've each done with it."

Another reason Beaton didn't wish to become intimate with Streisand was the same reason he didn't care to become overly familiar with other associates, such as Cukor with whom he finally didn't get on well. "Sometimes, in getting closer to somebody," he noted, "you find you have things in common. You get beneath the surface. But those same common traits or interests can, ironically, divide you. I'd rather have a good working relationship with someone like Miss Streisand than be a friend, mates, for a while, and less than friendly thereafter."

How did Beaton rate Barbra as a photographic subject?

"In a sense, she reminded me of Edith Sitwell, of whom I did some very famous, striking portraits towards the start of my career. Truly, there is nothing new under the sun, and all people are basically variations of each other. I tend to compare individuals, but only in terms of their being extraordinary. Both these women I mention were very simple, down-to-earth and blunt. Very evolved, in terms of their attitudes, actions, and reactions. Very willing to experiment. Willing to compromise, to a certain extent, but also adamant, in refusals.

"I found Barbra more beautiful in person than in the photographs I'd seen of her. To be honest, some of her outfits, for public consumption, were unflattering or vague. In person, her quality was better defined, and in rich clothes and colors, she came alive. The 'mod' look didn't favor her—it made her look rather an outcast, as though she were trying to conform to **their** standards. I felt her look, and her looks, had been compromised too often. She is an original, and needn't apologize for it.

"But her face, alone, without trappings to distract from it or clothes to categorize her, was really quite lovely. Classic proportions, in general, the only flaw being a bit of teenage acne, which rather gave her a more vulnerable, young look. I had seen photographs which made her look matronly, but in person, she was young-looking and -acting. Her nose wasn't as prominent as it would seem to be, as the camera emphasizes it.

"I cannot, and could not, understand the criticisms from certain quarters about her being homely, in the American sense of the word.

Now, I've worked with attractive, appealing actresses, and actors who were homely, or plain, even ugly. Nonetheless compelling. But Barbra had no ugliness about her. She could be made plain, in a natural, wholesome way, without her Cleopatra eye makeup; it's a pity her marvelous waif quality hasn't been allowed to show through more. The moviemakers seem to want to make her appear invulnerable, [and] invincible—which grows tiresome.

"I noticed a tendency towards overweight, which she had checked, and if it weren't for her discipline and immense personal resources, I could well imagine a double chin by age forty." Streisand turned forty on April 24, 1982, and still no double chin! "I really find it appalling, the way a perfect camera subject like Elizabeth Taylor let herself become unphotographable. But even before, while Miss Taylor may have been a more appropriate romantic leading lady, Barbra is a better photographic subject because of her facial sculpture, and the chameleon quality she exudes.

"Like many actresses, she believed she had a good and a bad side. Not so. The sides were different; few faces, fortunately, are symmetrical. Barbra's two sides simply had different planing, and her nose was less prominent on one side—the more beautiful side is the more prominent."

Asked where he would rate Streisand, among his diverse photographic subjects (some of the most intriguing of whom have been non-celebrities), Beaton paused before answering with measured consideration: "The classic face of all time, of

The Central Park filming of the future sequence in *On A Clear Day*. Costumes by Arnold Scaasi. FRANK TETI

course, belongs to Garbo [to whom Sir Cecil was nearly married—the only man ever to claim that distinction]. Not only, or so much, because of the face itself, which was perfect, but due to her ability to paint it with moods, attitudes, emotions, suggestions, . . . Dietrich's face was another camera dream, but more artificially so, more one-dimensional, and therefore less artistically valid.

"But Barbra's face is more varied than either woman's. Garbo's face flowed; it was not significantly different at slightly different angles. Barbra's is, markedly so, and has a faceted effect. That is, one hundred photos might not capture her essence, or define her as a subject and a human being. One lucky shot of Garbo might do it. Which makes for the better photographic subject? They are very nearly equally good, in differing ways. There is no clear-cut answer. Garbo and Streisand both had—rather, **have**, because the photographic tense is always **present**—remarkable intensity and honesty of feeling. What they express for the camera is not artifice, though both have good enough acting ability to make artifice work for the viewer, but is felt, at the moment, by them. Intensely felt.

"On a personal level, having known Garbo intimately, I would venture that this makes Barbra fascinating, wonderful to work with, difficult to know, and possibly more difficult and exasperating to know socially. Only the very complex or the very simple make marvelous subjects for photography or for costume design: a peasant in the Ukraine, a rice farmer in Burma, a Garbo, a Barbra Streisand. Not the proverbial house-wife-next-door, who might be simply complex to the point of stultification!"

How would Beaton rate other photographers' and designers' work with Streisand?

"An artist cannot pass judgment on another artist, for his—or her—own style will always seem the best and most natural. I have, however, seen some striking, marvelous stills of Barbra. Not from films; film stills rarely provoke interest, since they're far removed from real life and from the esthetic standards of some of the older, particularly period, pictures. Posed, I've seen her in breathtaking 'roles,' with imaginative if not technically brilliant costumes. Natural, she is more alive and her hair less of a vague molding. Photographers react to her with their cameras the way they react to her as a personality, or as a woman. Some capture her faults, or emphasize what they imagine to be faults and flaws; occasionally, in an improper light, she is unattractive or, worse, dull. Others capture the beauty, the girlishness, the pride, and womanly qualities, or the alien quality, or a look and period they impose upon her.

"By any standards, Miss Streisand is extraordinary. The camera is never indifferent to her, in a good photographer's hands. Her face alone or her personality alone, could fascinate. Together, they also captivate, in a positive sense. My compliment to the lady is that the more she is photographed, the more she ought to be photographed . . . ."

PAGES 65, 67, 73: CECIL BEATON, PAGES 66 AND 70: FRANK TETI, PAGES 68 AND 72: BOB DEUTSCH, PAGES 69 AND 71: MICHEL PARENTEAU COLLECTION

"Determined"

FRANK TETI

Frank Teti grew up in New York's Little Italy, went to Seward Park High School and taught himself photography. His pictures have graced the pages and covers of NEWSWEEK, LIFE, PEOPLE, US, TIME, McCALL'S, the VILLAGE VOICE, THE NEW YORK TIMES, and DAILY NEWS, as well as publications abroad such as BUNTE in Germany, PARIS-MATCH, OGGI in Italy, and the Brazilian MANCHETE. His work has also been in the books BARBRA: AN ILLUSTRATED BIOGRAPHY, ANN-MARGRET, BETTE MIDLER, and THE JOHN TRAVOLTA SCRAPBOOK.

KAREN MOLINE:
When did you decide you wanted to be a photographer?

FRANK TETI:
When I was about eleven years old, it seemed like every time my mother would take pictures, they would be off-center or out of focus, and my father wouldn't touch a camera. I said, "Give it to me!" I didn't want to be in the picture either; it wasn't just my mother's incompetence—which was an excuse—it was a combination of her not wanting to take the photos and me wanting to be on the other side of the camera.

So you're camera-shy. Would you hide if someone tried to take your picture?

Not necessarily. I'd project different attitudes. I'm a lot more confident in myself now than when I was eleven. The camera was my little shield that protected me.

When did you first sell a photograph?

I was thirteen or fourteen. A photo of Carol Burnett with her sister. It was in TV/RADIO MIRROR. I went there with an envelope that had these little snapshots in it. I said, "I want to see the editor!" and they let me in and she said, "Oh, I like this black and white. Will you sell it for $15?" And I said

(OPPOSITE) Backstage at the Academy Awards, April 14, 1969.

74

OK—I didn't know anything about money or anything like that. (Kind of like now!) After that I forgot about [it] for two years. And then one of the other photographers—Tony Rizzo—was running around telling everybody, "I just sold a picture of Alain Delon and his wife, to MOTION PICTURE magazine." I said, "Oh, really?" By this time I had a great portfolio together—slide-mounted photographs of Carol Burnett and Barbra Streisand from the Broadway show of FUNNY GIRL, and Elizabeth Taylor, and Richard Burton when he was in HAMLET. I went to MOTION PICTURE magazine, and made $625. The first person who bought my pictures was David Ragan. He was also the first who encouraged me. I was fifteen or so. Again, it was a necessity for me—I had just told my parents I wanted to go to California for awhile.

Why? Was this when you were in high school?

Yes. I wanted to see what it would be like in Los Angeles, and **be** the fantasy of television and motion pictures—see it live. My mother said make the money and you can go. And I made the money—it was very important for me to get it and I did. That was why I really started selling pictures.

Where do you sell most of your work now?

NEWSWEEK, PEOPLE, US. I've had three pictures in the "new" LIFE. I'd rather see one great photograph of mine appear every two or three months than have tons of pictures appear all the time.

Did you study photography anywhere?

The university of hard knocks: the streets.

You never had a teacher?

I've had a lot of teachers—just from picking up. I've never worked as an assistant to another photographer on a steady basis. I am absolutely in awe of Cecil Beaton's work. He's like Streisand. Not only was he a photographer, he was a set designer, a costume designer, a painter. He did so many things and he did them so well. It's the same thing with Streisand. She's gone from singer to Broadway star to movie star to songwriter to director. She's very bright, and she gets very disinterested after awhile and she likes a new challenge. That's interesting. I'm identifying with myself. When she first does something she's unsure, and then she gets better and better, and then she gets bored and goes on to something else. There's something that keeps her going—and keeps everybody else going. I think it's called **hope**.

When did you realize you could make a career of being a professional photographer?

I still haven't. I'm serious! When I graduated from high school, I had a choice of working in a bank or working for a photo agency (as a file clerk/slide mounter/gofer). I took the photo job; if you want to be a photographer, surround yourself with other photographers. If you want to be a criminal, surround yourself with other criminals. That's the only way you're gonna do it.

When you weren't at your job, who were you shooting?

I was patrolling Broadway at night. At 7 P.M. or 7:30, I'd go in front of Sardi's and around the theater district, and get photographs of whoever, going into shows. It was interesting. I sold most of the pictures to MOTION PICTURE magazine, TV/RADIO MIRROR. The movie magazines were coming out monthly, but now they're the PEOPLE and US magazines. There aren't so many.

Did they pay you well?

They paid very well. Going back to the mid-sixties, they were paying us $50 for a full-page color, when the going rate was $200. It was great for us and for them too. They had a smaller budget than PHOTOPLAY or MODERN SCREEN, but they did encourage us and always wanted to see our photographs. Dave and Larry Thomas were the editors, and they suggested certain directions for us. At one point, by the late sixties, for one of the magazines, they were paying us normal rates. It was $200 per color page and $400 for a black and white layout. We could do three or four pages of black and white and a color page in an afternoon for $600. And get two of these assignments a week. There weren't enough good photographers—and there was so much work that nobody wanted to do—shooting an afternoon of star with his wife and children. It was a lot of money.

And you were pretty young to be making that.

Oh sure. Eighteen, twenty, I was making a lot more then than I am now.

Then all of a sudden the economy turned around and magazines cut down because of the bulk paper rate and postage increases. Then the assignments were going down to $300 for a color and black and white, and it got real bad. After awhile I just said no, I won't do assignments for that little; I'm a legend in my own mind, and how dare they! But everybody did it—everybody went down in prices, and there were too many people who were starving that would do it.

You were more interested in shooting celebrities than reportage, it seems.

Then. I was into anything that shimmered under a spotlight. Television and media were so intriguing, seeing the celebrities. It was kind of my little world. Television more than anything else.

How did you meet Carol Burnett?

I went to the stage door. And there was Tony Rizzo, Santiago Rodriguez, and Bob Deutsch. We all first met at the stage door.

Were you waiting for autographs?

Only for the first couple of weeks. Autographs were getting real boring. The camera that I had used before was really crappy, so I begged and pleaded till I got a Brownie Starflash for $8 from my parents. Then I could compete with Tony and Bob and Santiago. Tony and I have had this rivalry for almost twenty years—it's like Hekyll and Jekyll.

What did Carol Burnett think when she would come out and see the four of you hanging out all the time?

Teti's first photo of Barbra as she leaves the stagedoor of *Funny Girl,* 1964.

She would just give us love. She was fabulous.

Did she get to know you personally?

She got to know us by our names. At that point we had lots of energy, and when you go through puberty, you get really crazy. It was the love we needed. It was real nice; she stopped and cared. And down the block, Streisand was rehearsing FUNNY GIRL.

You never saw Streisand in I CAN GET IT FOR YOU WHOLESALE?

No. I saw FUNNY GIRL the last few weeks of the run when I knew she would be leaving.

It seems you weren't as impressed with Streisand as you were with Carol Burnett.

Right. Not at all. As warm as Carol Burnett was, Streisand was very aloof. She was kind of the independent cat, where Carol Burnett was the loving puppy dog. (That's a strange way to put it.) I could never understand the fanatic image of Streisand, and her fans could never understand what I thought was so fantastic about Carol Burnett.

Many of the photographers I spoke to said that the first time they saw Barbra Streisand perform, they were mesmerized. You didn't feel that way?

I was curious about her. I thought her voice was nice. But when I first met her, I just didn't know what the fuss was all about. As I said, my camera has always been my introduction to meeting people, and also my shield to my adventures. I kind of blocked her out that way. I'm very aggressive in a lot of ways and I'm very shy in a lot of ways, but I'll go after whatever I want. I try to be as reserved as possible with my camera until I know the subject.

So you felt that way about Streisand and you didn't want to shoot her at first. When was the first time you saw her in person?

I can't say it was THE GARRY MOORE SHOW because I couldn't be bothered with her. She didn't impress me. We went to the Winter Garden Theater and we waited for her.

This was during the rehearsals for FUNNY GIRL.

Yes. At the stage door. She came out and ran into the car. And I said, "SMILE!" She went like this [grimaces], and I got a picture of her with a big smile; she's not looking into the camera.

She didn't talk to you?

No. I thought at that point that she was very much a snob, but I have the feeling she's very, very shy also. She couldn't understand after so many years what the big deal was about either. And I think it's the fact that she's so shy. Her being unavailable made people want to have more of her.

You also feel that you're very shy as well as aggressive. That sounds a lot like your description of Barbra Streisand.

Exactly. And I have the feeling that millions and millions of people feel the same way. There's something about her many people can identify with.

She's a superstar and she's not classically beautiful; she doesn't have the typical Hollywood face. She's got an incredible talent, but she doesn't look like you'd expect. She's got very human features and an offbeat manner—people relate to that whether she is singing or not. She's real; she's there.

She's the Great American Dream. Period. She's the ideal for a lot of people. Any movie that she's ever done, any book that's ever come out about her—anything **sells**.

When you first saw her did you think she was going to become the **superstar?**

No. Absolutely not. The only two people I've never thought would be as big as they became are Barbra Streisand and Barry Manilow. I knew Manilow would be a great songwriter, but I never thought he would be the **star** that he is. He was too skinny to be wearing white clothes with rhinestones and be in front of young girls. But he had it and he did it.

Let's go back to the FUNNY GIRL rehearsals.

We were still hanging out. Once the play was on, people were starting to go to the stage door and there were more crowds. I would either go late at night and know that Elliott Gould was going to go in the front of the theater instead of the backstage, so she could sneak out and get into the Mercedes.

They were already sneaking out at that point?

Yes. She's real good up to a point, and then she loses her patience.

In terms of being shot?

In terms of being clawed. She could never understand this whole thing. It's like you or me walking out of a building and all of a sudden people grab us: gimme your autograph, gimme your picture. This was her reaction; she just freaked.

And she hasn't stopped freaking since.

Of course it's gotten worse.

Were you selling your photographs of her at that point?

No, I was just doing it. I had so much energy and I was enjoying myself. She never really became all that big until 1968 when the movie FUNNY GIRL came out.

She was still a New York-based star; she wasn't yet international.

In New York you can be a real star—you can do something and really be appreciated. In Los Angeles you have to prove yourself.

You have two different media. Broadway stars in New York are unheard-of in California. But if you make a movie, everybody sees you. It's exposure. Streisand certainly would not have gotten the fame she did had she only done stage work. She couldn't have reached the audience.

But that's the only reason why she did the Broadway show—because she wanted to be a movie star. That was her goal. She didn't consider herself the singer, even though she's got a great voice, and she's more of a theatrical star. She very rarely does live performances now; she hates it with a passion.

She'll do benefits.

For something live, she's terrorized. I guess like anybody she prefers to do it three or four times.

She doesn't like to perform live and she's entitled to do what she likes.

Why not.

But on the other hand, she doesn't like to do things she doesn't have control over. She does a live performance; she can't control it—it is immortalized as it is. If she's on tape, she can re-edit, re-sync, be perfect. It points to the same thing: she doesn't want her photograph taken without her permission, and she won't sing if she doesn't have complete control. The audience is not going to see an instant replay.

So you and I are a lot more lucky than she is, because we have more control over our media than she does. That's one of the reasons I got into photography—because I can control it. I'd rather do a lot of assignments with **my** contacts—people I know—than get a magazine contact, because a magazine will see **all** of my photographs, whereas with a friend, I can edit the pictures. When David Ragan first bought my photos, he said, "Don't be the editor."

When was the last time you shot Streisand?

(OPPOSITE) In rehearsal for the Broadway *Funny Girl.* MICHEL PARENTEAU COLLECTION

It's been a long time. About five years ago at the opening of FUNNY LADY. It was absolutely wonderful and absolutely horrifying, like a lot of things. For the press conference in the morning, she arrived ten minutes early. There were big round tables, and she sat down at one and James Caan at another. She was very congenial and polite and professional. She answered all the questions for the press. Again, she mentioned how she'll walk out at the beach in Malibu and nobody will recognize her. I think it was Arthur Bell from the VILLAGE VOICE who said, "Oh really, why not, if you're such a big star?" And she replied: "People expect Barbra Streisand to have eyes this big and

be fifty feet tall." But here again, nobody would give you the satisfaction of knowing who you are in Hollywood. Later that evening was the premiere. It was a repeat of what happened at the premiere of HELLO DOLLY, which was **the** worst experience. The crowds were in a swell and three policemen were on each side and there were four thousand fans. The limousine pulls up and as soon as she gets out, the barricades break. Everyone starts screaming and carrying on. One section was set for the television crews, one for the still cameras. The podium falls, the curtain falls, there were people in front of her, people behind her. If she had been pushed she would have been dead. Something crazy happened.

That she sparks in people? When they see her they go crazy.

They only have to see her **hair**. It's not that she has to do anything.

What happened at the premiere of HELLO DOLLY?

That was the time she almost got trampled to death like in THE DAY OF THE LOCUST. The only other person besides her that I've ever seen nearly get killed at a premiere was Elizabeth Taylor. There was basically enough security, twelve policemen on each side of her; but the crowds are so freaked. A lot of flashbulbs went off as she arrived, still in the limousine on the street. That does attract attention—when you see the flashbulbs all go off near one car. Everybody gets really nervous. As soon as they pulled the car up, which took about five minutes, we all knew it was **the**

With James Caan at the
Funny Lady press conference.

Mob scene at the world premiere of *Hello Dolly,* New York, 1969.

car, and the barricades broke. Everyone was screaming.

How did she get into the theater?

With great difficulty. The police made a cordon and linked hands together. Her manager at the time, Marty Erlichman, got into a big fist fight with one of the DAILY NEWS press photographers. That was in the headlines. All of a sudden this glamorous facade—you know, Hollywood in New York—is put on. Ladies and Gentlemen, who's walking into the theater but Barbra Streisand! Everyone's in these gorgeous gowns and tuxedos. The theater lights are dimming, and all you can hear is: "Marty! Marty! Are you OK, Marty! What did they do to you! Marty!" Barbra was screaming down the aisles. He wasn't badly hurt, but you

don't expect to get your face punched-in at a world premiere of your client. It was so horrible. When the barricades break, some of the fans will go for the star, but most of them know what they want—to go into the theater. Once they're in there, they're gonna stay! Try to throw me out even if I am wearing a tee shirt. And it was still warm out; I think the reaction has a lot to do with the weather. It got **real** crazy.

Did you get into the theater, or shouldn't I ask!

Oh, of course. The photographers have to get their pictures, the writers have to get their stories, and security has to keep them out. Everyone panics and it turns into a great big mess. Streisand blew her cool. Instead of making this grand regal entrance, which she did later at the Pierre Hotel, she was really shaken by it. That I really feel sorry about.

How did your photographs come out?

I got some good ones. I sold them all over; everyone's sold from that night. Ron Galella got the best ones. I was a little bit to the side at all times and it shows in my pictures. But Ron was right dead center. Yet the premiere of FUNNY GIRL was my favorite experience of all. The New York premiere was very controlled. It was in October, and the weather was beautiful, and the crowds were enthusiastic but not crazy. A podium was set up in the middle of Times Square near the Criterion Theater where the movie was being shown. Across the street was a tent on what was then an empty lot. There were a lot of people—about two thousand, but the party went very smoothly. It was great. There was an admiration, not this type of clawing like the vultures, an animal lust.

Funny Girl world premiere and party, September 18, 1968.

Have you ever shot her at awards ceremonies?

At three of the Oscars: the year before she won, the year she won for FUNNY GIRL, and the year after. For FUNNY GIRL, she was like a little girl who has just won a doll. Her face was totally lit up and she was so excited. Of all the pictures of mine in this book, I have the fondest memories of those from that Oscar night. There was that magical moment of shooting photographs. Sometimes you just have a bad shoot like I did at HELLO DOLLY; I was thrown by the crowds and wanted to stay to the right to give her a little bit of space to get by. At the Oscars, though, I was incredibly enthusiastic. I shot half a roll of black and white (which appeared in TIME the following week), and I love about six frames of the color. I used a different lens and they're much tighter. I showed the pictures to her and she wanted copies of all of them. The color is in her house.

How did you get to show them to her?

At the filming of ON A CLEAR DAY YOU CAN SEE FOREVER. That's my favorite story. She was doing the scene in Central Park (in 1969) where she's wearing the zebra-type thing and the skull cap. I went over to her at the end of one of the takes, and I showed her the photos from the Oscars (she had just won a few months before). I asked her if she wanted a copy, and she said, "Which is your favorite?" I showed her one, and she said, "Well, why do you like this one and not this one?" What I analyzed later was that she was pointing to her famous left profile, which is the one she liked. The one I liked had her head turned towards the right, in profile, and I said, "Because you're happy." I really felt dumb saying that. I thought I should have come out with a clever answer. But that's exactly what it was. It doesn't matter if it's your left side or your right side or your hair's messed or you're freaked-out and beaming from some experience—it shows through everything else.

What was her response to that?

"I'll take a copy of all of them!" I sent them through her agent, two sets, so that she could sign a set for me. She signed all the Oscar photos, but she didn't sign the one at the party, which she had posed for. She was wearing the see-through dress, and she was leaning over and the face and the hands are great, but it was cut to her legs, and she was a little bit heavy in the stomach, and it really showed. She didn't like it so she didn't sign it. She's been OK to me.

That outfit was not flattering.

I didn't understand it, you know. Now her body is a lot better than it was then. She exercises. She's got the type of body—zaftig—which most of us have, and she gains weight very easily. That outfit really looked bad on her. Even if you had an incredible body, I don't think that outfit would really look good. It was designed by Arnold Scaasi for ON A CLEAR DAY. . . and it wasn't used. It was very expensive.

What do you think about her looks?

Her looks are classic—now.

(OPPOSITE) Party at the Beverly Hilton after the Oscars.

They weren't classic twenty years ago?

My tastes were different twenty years ago. Then, my favorite subjects were movie stars. Now my favorite subjects are my three cousins, Angela, Jennifer, and Thomas. What I'm shooting now that really turns me on would be Pope John II or a colorful lunatic in Greenwich Village, so long as somebody's giving some kind of energy. But the glamour has always been in my life. I really love the originality of somebody with their own style, whether it's Daffy Duck or Barbra Streisand. Streisand's individuality, her energy is what appeals to me most.

What do you think is her most striking physical characteristic?

Physical? I think her most striking characteristic is her personality. More than anything physical. I love her profile. I love her attitude. I hate her attitude. She reminds me a lot of having an older sister, where you want to love her and then at times she can really be such a perfectionist it just annoys you no end. And you have this kind of ongoing battle, which is what I feel Streisand has with the press. She absolutely can't live without the publicity, but she hates it.

It's become a no-win situation.

It depends on how you look at it. It just builds. I don't see her as often as I did at one particular point, but I have a lot more admiration for her, because of what she's done for herself.

She's intelligent enough to have somebody like Jon Peters with her, who's been incredibly helpful in her career and a good business-minded person. She's not going for somebody who's totally physical; it's kind of an even-type relationship.

Have you taken photos of the two of them together?

At the FUNNY LADY premiere—that was the only time. And the only time I shot her with Elliott Gould was at the premiere of FUNNY GIRL.

What about with the men she's dated.

Maybe Omar Sharif, but it wasn't at that particular point. I wasn't intrigued by the gossip about her, the stories of her with everybody in existence. Whether the stories were true, I don't know.

Have you seen her son Jason?

Well, I shot him about three months before he was born (laughs). Barbra was going into the Shubert Theater to see a play.

That doesn't count.

Her attitudes have changed drastically about Jason and photographs. At first she posed proudly with him—and now there's nothing.

Since you're more impressed with her mental attitude than her physical appearance, how do her clothes and appearance fit in? Does she try to project part of her personality through her clothes, making a statement?

Definitely. When she's not in the limelight she looks like hunger. The worst. But when she is in the limelight she's totally impeccable.

I happen to prefer her earlier style.

What changed her image was being on the best-dressed list and the worst-dressed list at the same time, 1964-65. In one of the first pictures I took of her she looks like she's—and this was a quote for the worst-dressed list—"She looks like someone in a getaway car." She had this cap on her head and a leather jacket.

When you succeed in Hollywood you have to be much more polished.

Which she knew. But at that particular point she was in the limelight wearing the go-go boots and the mini dresses, which still looked absurd. She learned later on, as she got to be about thirty, to wear more classical dresses and hairdos where, if you looked at it ten years from now, it still looks perfect.

She can look just as beautiful wearing a robe from a thrift shop as a ballgown. When you're younger you can get away with more.

Over sixty, she'll be able to get away with it again. You can get away with anything over sixty or under twenty.

Even fingernails that are claws?

Even so. She stated in an article that she let them grow to have people stay away from her. She was using her nails like I use my camera—as a protection.

(OPPOSITE) Exercising for *The Main Event*.   MICHEL PARENTEAU COLLECTION

I thought it was so she couldn't learn to type.

Oh sure. And she trimmed them to learn to play classical guitar.

Thinking back to all the celebrities you've shot, how do you rate Barbra Streisand among them: More difficult? Average? Or is she just incomparable?

I would say that she is a perfectionist. That for someone who's done what she's done, or is in demand as a Diana Ross or a Bette Midler, she's pretty well in the middle. She can be very difficult, but it's the demands on her.

You don't believe she overreacts?

Of course she overreacts. She loses her patience very quickly.

Have you ever had a really bad experience trying to shoot her?

No, but then of course I never let myself be in that situation. I realize that there are situations like that, but I would always not only be protected by my camera, but be protected by certain magazines, like NEWSWEEK, that I work for.

You have press credentials?

Yes. And I would only put myself in a situation—a press conference where there are only six other photographers—rather than doing a free-for-all at night.

When she sees she's about to be photographed, does she project a certain image—does she freeze and put on a "camera face?"

She's really not personally calculating. Professionally, she's calculating, but as a person, no, she is very open and honest. And real quick-tempered too. So, she's got many moods, and you can just shoot five different frames in the middle of a situation, and have five different people. She's got a very animated face. With each mood her face changes and it's like seeing another person.

Other photographers have said that when she sees a camera, she goes blank, or she tries to hide.

That's funny. If she was ever like that, it was at the beginning (during FUNNY GIRL rehearsals) when she didn't understand why people would want to take pictures of her walking around.

What's the one word or expression you'd use to describe her?

Determined. I think she was very determined—and a lot more determined earlier in her career than now. The whole trip of being unpopular in school because of her appearance, her clothing, because she had to be an original; she **had** to be different so she made herself very weird-looking. She made people goof on her—that kind of energy. So all of a sudden people were just grabbing her, pawing her in all these different directions. It's really difficult. Everyone just sees the highlights—your family, your friends—they don't see the work you've put in.

With Streisand, it's a very ambivalent feeling. You admire her and yet

At a benefit for the
Bedford-Stuyvesant restoration
project, Americana Hotel, 1972.

you have terrible problems trying to get a simple photograph.

To do it now I would not go through the same situation. Definitely not. I would do something where it's controlled or through the press.

Well, you've already done it; you get pushed so many times before you say: that's it. Do you think YENTL is going to be a success?

Personally, no. But I've been wrong with her a lot of times, so I don't know.

What has been her biggest career mistake?

The movies UP THE SANDBOX and ALL NIGHT LONG. Those are the only movies that did not have the character role of Streisand. Any movie that she does that is Barbra Streisand will

work. So if YENTL is very Barbra, then it will succeed, but if it's not—you just don't know. Everything she's done so far has made so much money. Because she's been **Barbra Streisand**.

She has an excellent conception—probably better than any other star of her caliber (which is one reason she's a star of course)—of what she projects to people and she chooses roles that especially project that kind of ability. You don't even have to describe what her image is, but when you say "Barbra Streisand," everyone reacts the same way.

There are certain formulas that are guaranteed, and there are others that are challenges. Some actors will do one role and then go totally different—and it'll work—like Dustin Hoffman in THE GRADUATE and MIDNIGHT COWBOY, whereas somebody else could do movies and one is great and the next is a bomb.

Streisand has an image of perfection in her head. People expect a certain level from her and they won't let her fall below it.

She won't let herself fall below it.

The public won't either.

Definitely not. If she wants, she says too bad, and she doesn't do another movie for years. She can take her time. She knows what she can do and can't do.

Is there something she hasn't done that you think she wants to?

Oh, I'm sure—and she'll try to do it, whatever it is. That's what I admire about her. If she falls, she falls, but she's **gonna do it**. Nobody's ever remembered for something they're **gonna** do—you just go ahead and do it. You stop talking about it. She's the same way.

Just more visible.

A lot more. Yet she's been hiding in the last year and a half—she's only been photographed twice, by Greg Gorman. That was for her album cover and LADIES' HOME JOURNAL. For fifteen minutes, with the frizzed hair. She's not even spending enough time every once in a while to be photographed.

You mean posed photo sessions?

Yes, and she's also getting more and more scarce on public outings. It makes the market more crazy; you've got to use the same photographs.

Why does Barbra hate being photographed so much?

She doesn't have total control over it. She **does** have total control over the Scavullo pictures, but then again they're for publicity purposes. The rumor is that he got $50,000 to $100,000 for each shooting (THE MAIN EVENT and A STAR IS BORN). I would definitely want total control then!

But don't you think she makes it more difficult—if the market were flooded people wouldn't bother her when she went out.

I don't think **she** thinks about that. She's kind of beyond it. There would never be enough. There would be so many people hounding her for a period of time, the supply and demand economics, that it would drive her nuts. She wouldn't do it. If she stood up on a bridge and was photographed by every photographer in the world, they would leave her alone for at least five minutes. And then they would bother her again. I don't think there would ever be enough film to stock.

Yet how many superstars are there on her level—to shoot?

Exactly. How many people can relate to Jackie Onassis? **Everybody** can relate to Barbra Streisand. There is a great classic thing with blue-blooded people. Their attitude is that you always bring people up to your level, you never go down to theirs. Whereas Streisand (like me) will always go down to somebody's level if she's really pissed.

You must have seen her like that.

Oh yes. It was my most embarrassing experience with her. We were all waiting for Elizabeth Taylor and Richard Burton at the Plaza Hotel. It was a fundraising benefit for the American Cancer Society in the mid-sixties. Streisand was in FUNNY GIRL on Broadway, and hadn't made the movie yet. Burton was in HAMLET. Anyway, we were waiting on the 58th Street side—there's a Fifth Avenue side and a 59th Street side—but very few people come out on 58th Street. There's an area there

(OPPOSITE) *Funny Lady* press conference, 1975.

Arriving for a fashion show
by designer Valentino at
the Pierre Hotel, 1972.

with glass doors. All of a sudden, the glass doors opened up, and who comes out but Barbra Streisand and Elliott Gould. She sees that there are maybe about five or six photographers, some fans with cameras, and a couple of people waiting for autographs. Basically the kids would wait around. So she said, "Come on, Elliott, let's run. They want to take my picture!" One of my friends really freaked, and ran up to her, doing this halftime trot next to her, going, "Listen, honey, we're not here for **you,** we're here for the **real** star, Elizabeth Taylor. NOW YOU'RE GONNA POSE!" She stopped and she did pose for him. It was crazy. I wasn't taking photos. She had her mouth open. She knew that if she didn't pose she was not going to get away from this one.

I'm sure she was frightened. He was so pissed that she had the balls to run away, like everybody was going to attack her.

So he went and nearly attacked her!

You want it, you're gonna get it. But the last laugh was on him, because she really knew **she** was going to be the greatest star. At that particular point I never thought anybody could replace Elizabeth Taylor—but Streisand did. Somebody's going to replace Streisand too, eventually. I'll be curious to see who it is. It's time: Streisand came in at about twenty-five and now she's forty, phasing-out. There's some sort of set pattern. Whether it's the movie industry backing you for millions of dollars or you do it yourself. Somebody like

Carol Burnett is able to be as nice as possible, because she's had a husband who could say no for her. Same thing for Ann-Margret. They bring out a lot of love, but they have people around them that do speak for them. But Streisand is always saying no for herself.

Jon Peters says no for her.

I'm sure that makes her less irritable than she was in her earlier career. But does he really?

Actually, I think Streisand is too much of her own personality to let anybody talk for her.

Jon Peters gives her a run for her money. Which she needs—she needed a stong man, and he is.

Does Barbra recognize you at all or remember you as an early fan?

Yes. There have been times where she'll go, "Hi, how ya doing." She'll point to me. It depends if there are a lot of people around, or if she's relaxed, or whatever. She's more sincere than a lot of celebrities. And there are a lot of celebrities that are much warmer, that'll run up to you or whatever. But she's not two-faced, or an eager beaver. She's not, "Oh hi, my best friend" one minute and, "Go to hell" the next. That reminds me of the time at the Tony Awards where she won a special Tony. It was her fourth award that year—she had already won the Oscar, the Emmy, and the Grammy. She's a big deal, and they're not bringing her across the street to Sardi's. I was covering it for NEWSWEEK, and I **had** to get a photograph of her with the Tony or what-

ever. I knew the party was going to be at the Waldorf-Astoria. I rushed over, and spotted a girlfriend of hers, named Sissy. And I called out, "Sissy, where's Barbra?" Sissy was stunned, because she didn't know who the hell I was. She froze, and the first thing I see is Marty Erlichman (waving his hands) going, "No pictures." And then I hear, "No Marty, let him take a picture, let him take a picture." And I got this picture. She was so frightened.

Of you or the situation?

I have no idea. I did **not** see her! I don't know how she managed to get in the same room where I could not feel the radiation—which I can do. I only spotted her girlfriend. It depends on your presence, the way you carry yourself.

What's your favorite shot of Barbra?

They're all my favorites.

"A Perfectionist to a T"

YANI BEGAKIS

has been three-time President of The Foreign Press Association—also known as the Golden Globes. His photographs have appeared in magazines throughout the world. Born in Turkey, he moved to Los Angeles in 1959, and has remained there ever since. Yani has been a veteran of the scene in Hollywood for over twenty years, and serves as a father-figure, inspiration, and role model for the younger generation of photographers in Los Angeles.

<u>KAREN MOLINE:</u>
Tell me how your career began.

<u>YANI BEGAKIS:</u>
When I came to Los Angeles, I was working for a small newspaper back home in Istanbul, Turkey. Then I was assigned to work for a Japanese publication in 1959, and as a requirement I became a photojournalist—it was stories as well as pictures. So I joined the Hollywood Foreign Press Association. I have been President three times, Executive Secretary six times, Treasurer one time, Chairman of the Board two times, and a Member of the Board four times. For each of Barbra's movies, there would be a setup, posed shooting for the press, on the set. She was always very nice, very accomodating. She always says hello to me.

You've mainly shot her at press functions. Do you ever take pictures of her out in public, at restaurants, for example?
No, I don't frequent many restaurants. Unless it's a press-oriented function, normally I don't go to restaurants. I guess in the early part of her life in Los Angeles, I used to see her. The Press Association had an office in the Ambassador Hotel.

(OPPOSITE) Backstage at the Academy Awards, April 10, 1968.

When she first came out here with El-liott Gould, she was very aloof. No-body bothered her that much unless it was opening night. So she used to go out and shop and buy clothes and so forth. Then when she became fa-mous people started bothering her, and she shied away from a lot of things.

Would you have your camera with you then?

Not all the time. I don't follow peo-ple with a camera. I only carry it when it's necessary. I do my work, and when it's my work I carry my camera. I'm also a human being, and I have this other position [at the Press Associa-tion], so I cannot be chasing people out. I would never classify myself as a paparazzi. I respect the profession and I respect the people I shoot for. I have a good name in this town and everybody knows me and every-body says hello. Sometimes, I'm in-vited to homes for private parties. No cameras. I keep the two separate, you know.

If you're a paparazzi, you take your camera with you all the time.

It makes a big difference—the be-havior and the way you address peo-ple. They consider you accordingly. So, naturally picture-taking is a large part of my life, as I said: I'm a photo-journalist. I became a photojournalist because all the publications I work for, and the screen magazine in Ja-pan, require a lot of pictures be out each month. I have to prove that I am there [at functions] and so forth.

Are you paid well?

Oh yes, I'm very happy. I have a comfortable life, I must say.

What was your initial impression of Barbra the first time you shot her?

The first time I shot her in Los Angeles was the night she opened the Coconut Grove. After her big hit in New York and San Francisco, she came into L.A. Opening night was re-ally a superstar event. She wore that navy dress. She was very accommo-dating and very willing to cooperate with everybody. She stayed in the hotel for about two weeks. She was very like a little girl, on her own. With her husband, Elliott Gould at the time, she used to go down to the shops by the hotel and stroll around. Because nobody very much bothered her.

Photographers in New York said that when she was on Broadway, she'd walk to the theater and back, and nobody would much bother her. That didn't happen until she became really famous.

The famous navy dress, 1965.
(OPPOSITE) A portrait for *Hello Dolly*.

100

MICHEL PARENTEAU COLLECTION

Then she made FUNNY GIRL—of course she had done the television specials, which put her up. But after the first film, she won an Oscar right away. Naturally the pressure gets bigger and bigger and bigger when you reach the plateau of superstar. And at the time, there were not as many paparazzis as there are now. Today it's impossible; you don't even have to be a superstar to be bugged to death. Anybody off the streets becomes a photographer, and the scene has changed tremendously. Even a few years later, when HELLO DOLLY premiered in New York. . .

There was a riot.

. . .a flashbulb went [off] in her eye and she got so scared and frightened. We had her here at the HELLO DOLLY premiere, and they brought her out and she posed on the set. On the set, they had thousands and millions of extras, and everybody watched her doing the parade number—and nobody bothered her. I was always on the sets when Barbra made movies. Five or six of them . . . with Robert Redford, and so on.

There were never any problems, were there?

No.

People just doing their jobs.

On the set, of course, because of union rules, you can't take your cameras. You just go and observe **her**. She was never that reclusive to say, "Don't let anybody come near me," I must say.

What do you see as her most striking characteristic?

I would say she is very smart.

What about her appearance?

Well, my mother used to say, and you can quote my mother, who didn't speak English, she's "the lady with the fingernails." I think it's her uniqueness, her face. It's her. She has a large nose, but that doesn't necessarily make her ugly.

I think it makes her more beautiful.

It gives her the Grecian beauty.

Are you Greek?

Yes. It gives her the Grecian beauty because the Greek goddesses have this sort of look the way Barbra has. She has a unique face; you can recognize her instantly. Whereas you can see a hundred other beautiful girls and you don't recognize any of them. That all adds to it.

What do you think about her clothes?

When she goes out publicly, to functions and all, she seems to dress accordingly. On the sets, of course, when she makes the movies, she has to wear what the designers make for her, and they're always well done. The clothes she wore in FUNNY GIRL were exquisite, as in HELLO DOLLY. When she goes out informally, she goes informal!

Is there a particular way that she's ever dressed that you especially remember?

The classic profile.

Oh yes. One time she was doing an ED SULLIVAN SHOW in Las Vegas and she opened at the International Hotel. I thought that hairdo and the way she dressed was beautiful.

What did she look like?

She was wearing a pink outfit and her hair was rather light—it was not the dark hair that Barbra has had—it was rather blondish-light, and it was done so beautifully. She looked like a Greek goddess that night. I will never forget that look when she was on that stage to sing. When they were taping it I happened to be there, and I photographed her on stage. And then I went backstage and she was there with Eydie Gormé and Steve Lawrence—they had come to see her. I was the only photographer there and I just took a few pictures; I didn't bother them. She didn't say, "Oh, that's enough," or anything. I was there to do the thing and she was very nice about it. That's why I always have nice things to say about Barbra.

I'm glad, because she's been difficult for a lot of people.

Yes, I know, I know. She has been difficult, but. . . .

Do you feel that she's any more difficult than any other star of her caliber?

Not necessarily. There have been other difficult stars as well. As I said, she keeps her private life private, but when she has to do something in regard to publicity, she has been extremely cooperative.

Do you have a favorite shot of Barbra?

There are a few shots that I have not been able to find. The one from Las Vegas, not the black and white, which I have, but there is a color shot somewhere along the way, either in my apartment or on some editor's

desk. It's really exquisite, and I wish I could find it. Like I said, she looks like Aphrodite or Venus de Milo. She's absolutely ravishing in that shot.

How about your experiences shooting her. What was the best and the worst?

The worst was being pushed and shoved by other photographers when she took Jason to the screening of WILLY WONKA AND THE CHOCO-LATE FACTORY. It was the worst situation for her and for me because the other photographers made it such a difficult situation to shoot her. The best, I still say, was that Vegas taping when I was the only one there.

She couldn't have been more coop-erative, backstage in the dressing room with her show business friends. And she was delightful. That's why I say that when she moves me out in a crowd and she says hello, it all de-pends on the rapport you have be-tween these people. And I have this rapport with a lot of other stars, Most of them know me by my first name, and they single me out when they come to the Oscars.

Were you at the Oscars when Barbra won for FUNNY GIRL?

Oh yes. At the Oscars, we are backstage, and she came and posed when she won. Naturally we had

Ed Sullivan Show
in Las Vegas, 1969.
One from Begakis'
sequence of his
favorite photos.

watched on television as well. She
was extremely delightful about it.

Did she say anything that you remember?

Not in the photo room. I do remember the Golden Globes when she was winning for FUNNY GIRL. She kept winning—four Golden Globes—back and forth, back and forth. I kept saying to her, "You're going to come back one more time," because she was Best Actress, Best Song, Best Picture, Comedy and Musical. And she'd say, "I hope I will, I hope I will!" She couldn't have been more bubbly than that night; the bubbliest Barbra

Streisand I have ever seen. She was
like a little child.

She doesn't strike me as being that kind of person.

She was very bubbly. She kept jumping up and down.

Have you ever shot her with the men in her life?

Yes, with Ryan O'Neal—but not very much. One night we got a tip that she was going to a screening of a preview with him. And then with Jon Peters, many times. Jon also knows me and he'll point me out to her, so if they're in a kind of rush, they'll stop.

105

When she was shooting A STAR IS BORN, they had a press junket. She was extremely friendly to everybody. They had about three hundred to five hundred press from all over the country and the world. And don't forget she was working at the same time, shooting, doing production and the big number in the open-air field. She couldn't have been nicer.

Do you have one particular word or expression to describe Barbra?

I have to think of the right word. She is a perfectionist to a **T**. Yes, a perfectionist. She knows exactly what she wants.

Some photographers have said that she likes to be shot from her left side.

I never had that request from her.

She just sees you, says hello, and lets you do what you want?

Right. She's a marvelous business lady and she does what she wants; she knows what she's doing. Basically she's a very shy girl who has become very famous. Where I see her, she is shy. That's my version of Barbra Streisand.

Backstage at the Las Vegas Hilton. L-R: Pat Boone, Steve Lawrence and Eydie Gormé.

(OPPOSITE) Barbra presenting the Oscar for Best Actor to John Wayne for *True Grit* on April 7, 1970.

"The Greatest Voice I've Ever Known"

TONY RIZZO

A Hollywood photographer, Tony Rizzo is a transplanted New Yorker who began shooting stills of the stars when he was eleven and sold his first picture when he was fourteen. His photographs have appeared in NEWSWEEK, TIME, TV GUIDE, US, PEOPLE, PHOTOPLAY, and LADIES' HOME JOURNAL, as well as the LONDON SUNDAY MIRROR and other foreign publications.

On the other side of the lens, Mr. Rizzo has appeared in three films including THE DAY OF THE LOCUST, numerous television shows such as THE NIGHTSTALKER, and TV commercials. A frequent talk-show guest (he has been on A.M. LOS ANGELES five times), Tony has also been a staff writer and photographer for SOAP OPERA DIGEST for the past five years, and a former columnist/writer for PHOTOPLAY.

At work on a forthcoming novel and a major project for MGM-TV, Tony Rizzo, in addition, acts as a personal manager for a range of clients.

KAREN MOLINE:

When did you begin your career as a photographer?

TONY RIZZO:

When I was eleven years old, I used to hang out at the candy store on Second Avenue and 12th Street. Right next door was the Phoenix Theater (now Entermedia), a very prominent Off-Broadway theater. I met Carol Burnett there—she was playing ONCE UPON A MATTRESS. And I'd go up to Studio 50 to see her on THE GARRY MOORE SHOW. She would get me her house seats. We'd go out for a Coke between the dress rehearsal and the taping, and she'd cue me for the response—audiences need to be led!—there were no overhead cues for laughter, only applause. Well, one night, during the opening number of GARRY MOORE, all the cast and stars came riding out on a golf cart, including Robert Goulet and Barbra Streisand. She looked very unusual to be a star. We still didn't know who she was. She did her first number standing in the window of a set of a house, singing "When The Sun Comes Out." When she finished, the audience gave her a standing ovation for twenty minutes. In the second half, she sang "Happy Days." Later, they said that she was appearing in I CAN GET IT FOR YOU WHOLESALE, so I left the audience and ran up to the Shubert Theater. I snuck in for the second half (which is when she had her big number as Miss Marmelstein). I fell in love with her immediately. At

(OPPOSITE) At the Oscar party, Beverly Hilton Hotel, 1970. Rizzo's favorite shot.

that time, I used to run around looking for stars. I'll tell you a little-known fact: Carol Burnett was offered FUNNY GIRL first. She turned it down and suggested Barbra Streisand.

Were they friends?

Well, Barbra was on her show and Carol was impressed with her talent. Through Carol Burnett I met all these stars, and I decided I had to have pictures of them. I bought a Brownie Starflash. I was taking pictures all the time. I started with black and white and went to color. I got to meet all these people: I'd go to the hotels where they were staying and I'd call them up on the house phones and say, "Hello, Miss Garland, this is a fan of yours and I'd like to know when you are coming down so I can get your autograph." And she'd say, "Oh, about nine o'clock." And she'd come down at eleven. She was always late.

Is that how you got to know Barbra Streisand?

I got to know her because I knew Carol Burnett.

What was the first picture you took of Barbra?

I saw her backstage and said, "Can I take your picture?" and she said, "Oh, I look terrible," but I took it anyway. It was so bad I threw it out. One day in the doorway of Korvettes on Fifth Avenue, she was there with Elliott Gould, and she introduced him to me as "My fiancé." I called up Earl Wilson at the POST and he ran it in his column. Anyway, when I was fourteen, my parents thought it was sick that I was chasing after movie stars. They said, "You want to be an actor, we'll give you acting lessons, but taking pictures is disgusting." So they cut my allowance. Four dollars a week. I needed the money, so I went to all the movie magazines, and the last one I called, MOTION PICTURE magazine, bought my first photograph. A full-page in color.

How much did they pay?

$75, which was a lot of money in 1962.

But were you basically doing photography to spite your parents or did you see it as a serious hobby?

It was a way to get away from home. But it was much more for the camaraderie; there was a clique of us who hung out together. When I was seventeen, I joined the Navy, and while I was stationed in Washington, D.C., the base was right next to the radio station where all the stars went to give interviews when they were in the area. I would take photos there on weekends and when I got passes. I put myself through the Navy. When I was seventeen, I also made my first trip to California for the Academy Awards (for TV/RADIO MIRROR magazine) and the following year I covered the Emmy Awards. After the Navy, I decided to move to California (in 1968)—I was nineteen.

And on October 17, 1968—I remember that date well—I was covering the discotheques. (I wasn't doing well at all; I was starving as a matter of fact. But even though I went to press events where there was plenty of food, I never ate because the

(OPPOSITE) Barbra and the Emmy for her first television special *My Name is Barbra*. New York Hilton, September 12, 1965.

press corps had such a bad reputation for that. You never saw a photo of me with a fork in my mouth.) So I was shooting a screening of a Steve McQueen movie. Barbra Streisand and Elliott Gould were there with Terry Leff and Abbe Lane. As they were leaving, Barbra kept hiding her face, and Elliott was dragging her away. Three other photographers and myself were following them, trying to get a shot. Barbra kept saying, "You have enough! You have enough!"—even though we didn't have anything at all. And I said, "If you had been polite and stopped for us, we wouldn't have to bother you now." Elliott lunged forward and grabbed the chain of my camera and began to choke me. He was choking me with the chain of my own camera. He said, "I'll break your camera, you son-of-a-bitch!!" And I said, "Watch your mouth, there are ladies present." He then threw me down in the gutter, against a parked car. As a result, I dislocated my shoulder and did damage to my back and neck. I still can't hold a camera steady without a tripod. I was out of work for three months. I filed suit and it got to court three years later. That was June of 1971. Gould was found guilty on all three charges of battery. And the judge—while Gould was on the witness stand—asked him for his autograph. Right **after** that, the judge pronounced him guilty. I was awarded $6,501 in damages. As we were walking out of court, Gould said to me, "I hope you can go far on that."

He was being sarcastic?

He told reporters, "This is funnier than all my movies." They asked him if he thought it was fair. His lawyer dragged him away before he could say anything.

You must have been happy about the verdict?

Of course I was happy. I won. Now all the other members of the press corps can take pictures without being bullied by the actors. Once we were out of court, Elliott Gould walked over to me. I said, "I hope you understand it's a matter of precedent and principle," and I extended my hand. He said, "I hope you know why I can't do that." And he walked away, over to the camera crews. He told them, "The joke's on him. I don't have the money." That was broadcast on the news and I got a check two days later. Now he's always nice to me if we see each other.

You saw him often after that?

The next time I saw him was about a year later. I was in a little restaurant, and I was trying to get out of the place, but he was sitting at a table near the doorway. I saw him there, and was hoping he'd finish before I did. But I had an appointment, and had to leave, so I went to the cash register, and I heard him say to the man with him, "Hey, ain't that the Rizzi character?"

He called you Rizzi?

Yes, and I thought, Oh God, what do I do—should I go out the front door or look for the back door. But I looked him right in the eye and said, "Hi, how

With
Elliott Gould,
1968.

you doing," and walked out the door. The next time I saw him was about six months later at a screening of LENNY, in Westwood. Though the snack bar was closed, I was standing near it, and I heard someone come in behind me and say, "It's that guy who wins lawsuits against me." I turned around, and there was Elliott Gould facing me, with his elbow on the counter, leaning on his knuckles, you know, and he smiled at me. I said, "How you doin', Elliott," and turned and walked away. The next time was at a party in Beverly Hills. I walked in, and was standing on this sort-of elevated platform and he came racing toward me. Everybody thought he was going to hit me, but he said, "How ya doing!" He shook my hand; he was really friendly.

Do you think he acted that way because there were so many other people around?

No, I think he wanted to get it over, something of the past.

The incident was quite a while ago.

But you see, I was the injured party in the sense that when it happened, Barbra had approval of a cover for COSMOPOLITAN magazine, and they had selected one of my pictures, from FUNNY GIRL. When she found out who the photographer was, she had it pulled. And they killed the story as a result of that too. That was hard. It would have been a great credit to have a COSMO cover.

Did the incident hurt your business because people saw you as a liti-

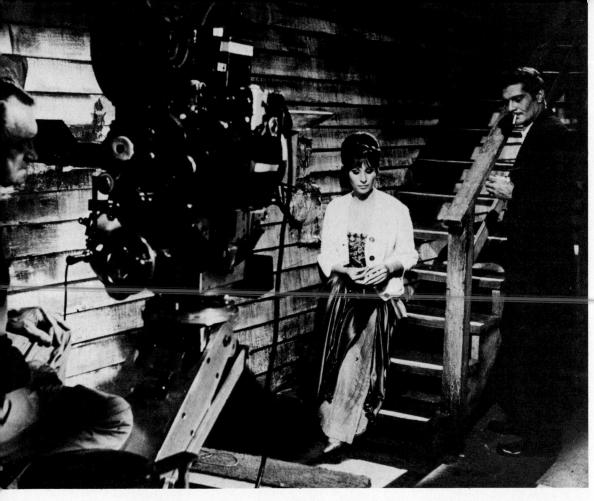

On the *Funny Girl* set
with Omar Sharif.
MICHEL PARENTEAU COLLECTION

gious photographer, or did they feel sorry for you?

They made fun of me for years. "Oh there he is—anybody hit you up this week? Ha ha ha."

That's horrible.

Yes, that was one of the big points of the trial. I was embarrassed publicly. It was in all the trade papers; on the front page of the HOLLYWOOD REPORTER: "Tony Rizzo Wins Suit With Gould." Streisand, after the first day in court, was removed from the suit because she didn't actually hit me.

Did she remember you as the person who used to hang out and be a big fan?

I don't know. I really don't know. I don't think she paid enough attention to remember. You know, I was thinking, very carefully, about giving you a statement about why Streisand acts the way she does in public. And I came to a very good conclusion. On FUNNY GIRL, Streisand's first movie, she was reported to have ten or twelve cinematographers fired, because she had to be photographed a certain way, to her liking.

Her left side?

Well, one side is for comedy, and one side is for everything else. When she goes out to a public event, she wants to minimize the amount of still pictures taken of her that she has no control over. So, she hides. Or people date her to protect her. After Elliott Gould, Ryan O'Neal got into a scuffle with photographers, Jon Peters scuffled with photographers. Anyone she's ever gone out with has had to **protect** her. From what, I don't know. Having her picture taken? And I think it's because she feels that she can't control what she is going to look

114

like so she doesn't want **anything** taken. In the sense of promotion— she's protected and hidden and guarded—it works to her advantage.

Sure, people always want something that's unavailable. Is it ego about her appearance or just fear?

I don't think she likes the way she looks in photographs when she doesn't have control over them.

Do you think she likes the way she looks in photographs she DOES have control over?

I'm sure she likes them. I've seen fabulous pictures of her.

Which is the favorite photograph of her that you've taken?

One of my favorite pictures was taken at the Academy Awards. She's sitting at a table, in a party outfit, with a pillbox hat. It's a very pensive study of Streisand, and I think of her as a serious artist. Most of the work she's performed in **is** serious. Even FUNNY GIRL. I did like her in THE OWL AND THE PUSSYCAT and in A STAR IS BORN.

Yes, I liked her in that too. I always felt that despite how contrived the plot was, she was the best part of it.

She made sure of that! The scene where she is running from the photographers at the awards—the Grammy Awards—no photographer, in reality, would really be allowed inside the room where the TV cameras are. The photographers would all be in the back rooms, the press rooms.

She put that scene in as an attack on photographers?

Yes, I think so. That's how **she** sees photographers. And in one scene, Kris Kristofferson pushes a news commentator—remember? That's also Streisand.

I wonder if she's basically a nice person.

I don't know her as a person; I only know her as a talent. And I only know her as a lady on the run.

Does how you feel about her talent override what you feel about her as a person?

Let's put it this way. I feel flattered that Barbra Streisand won't speak to me. It means she had to speak to me once. It's a distinction!

Did she ever tell you that she liked your photography?

Well, she liked my COSMO shot; that's why she wanted to know who the photographer was.

You know, you've got a completely different way of thinking about Streisand than the other photographers I've talked to for this book. Most see her as way up there on a pedestal, unapproachable, but you've had this unfortunate kind of direct contact with her.

I'll tell you how I feel about her performance: I think she's probably the greatest talent of all times. I feel very lucky to have photographs of her as I do. But as a person, I think she must be terribly unhappy, because she finds herself in a kind of prison—a minimum security prison where she is isolated from the rest of the world. She cannot walk among the people. She would not be comfortable walk-

Different looks, 1964.

ing among the people. And when she goes out in public it's an ordeal for her. And I sympathize with her. I really feel sorry for her. I mean, in a sense it's over-paranoia. One of my greatest dreams when I was younger and hoping to be an actor, was to work with Barbra Streisand, but I know now it will never happen. So . . . I just have a tremendous respect for her talent and her and I feel very sad about how her life has gone.

What do you think about the direction she's taking with YENTL?

I once talked to William Wyler, who directed FUNNY GIRL. I congratulated him for winning the Academy Award, and he said, "Well, I didn't really direct that picture."

I didn't think William Wyler would ever admit to something like that.

He did laugh when he said it.

I've heard that she was even directing I CAN GET IT FOR YOU WHOLESALE. And she was a complete unknown then.

She's always had her ideas about how things are to be done. They went through a lot of changes in FUNNY GIRL—and most of her judgment was correct. At least about **her** talent.

Even if one is singleminded and goes about a career in what could be called a peculiar manner, she certainly knows what she's doing.

I think the one thing Streisand has to learn, though, is ensemble acting. Everything she does is a one-woman show. She's in charge. When she came out to Hollywood, I once got on a set. Tom Nardini, [who] was in CAT BALLOU with Jane Fonda, was under contract at Columbia. He took me there to the shooting of FUNNY GIRL. And I got kicked off with him because we didn't have badges on and she made everyone wear badges on her show.

Whenever she came out to a party or a premiere, it was always a big to-do. She came to the opening of THE WILD ROVERS, which was a Ryan O'Neal picture, when she was dating him. It was at Grauman's Chinese. They came in [through] a side entrance, and they sat near the back door of the theater and were taken out the back door. We had to fight to get any pictures at all.

Who do you shoot for now?

Myself. SOAP OPERA DIGEST magazine. I'm one of their leading writers and photographers; I do most of their West Coast work.

Tell me what you think about Barbra's appearance. Have you seen her change over the years?

When I saw Barbra Streisand in Shubert Alley when she was doing WHOLESALE, she used to be led around by her mother and Barbra used to wear a bun on top of her head, and very drab, second-hand clothes. Then when she did FUNNY GIRL, she used to dress in jeans and motorcycle jackets, and things. I think her appearance [is a] marked difference. Her looks are more classic. She's got more money and more control, and more taste. She dresses much nicer—she always dresses very well—although people thought that what she wore the year that she won the Oscar was godawful.

What do you consider to be her most outstanding characteristic?

Her voice.

Anything physical?

Her nose. That goes without saying, doesn't it? I've always been fascinated by her nose, because I have a big nose myself. But I have been fascinated by the way her nose has changed over the years.

Has it really changed?

Look at her early pictures and look at her most recent pictures, and you can tell the difference. When I was a guest on THE STEVE ALLEN SHOW, I showed pictures of the stars. And when I showed early Streisand and more recent Streisand, they made me go back and forth. They commented on how she looks as though she's had a nose job.

When were you on THE STEVE ALLEN SHOW?

I think it was 1971. I was on [as a guest] showing slides of some of my pictures and talking about the stars. I had the highest rating they ever had in Los Angeles.

When was the last time you shot Barbra Streisand?

At the Academy Awards with John Wayne.

That's been a few years.

Yes—I haven't seen her much. She's been hiding, more or less. I was invited to go to the location shooting of A STAR IS BORN in Arizona, but they changed their minds, thinking that Streisand might be offended that she would be paying for me to go there . . . .

Have you ever noticed her fingernails?

She has very, very, long fingernails. I would not want to be caught in an alley with her. That reminds me of a story. She went to a screening of WILLY WONKA AND THE CHOCOLATE FACTORY, and she brought her son Jason along. When she was leaving she came out the back way and all the photographers got at the foot of the staircase where she had to go down. But I went onto a service porch, which was off to her side. I got pictures of her from the back with all the other photographers as a backdrop. And at one point she turned around and said to her son Jason, "Stick out your tongue at the awful man." He turned around and stuck out his tongue at me.

That's terrible! She must have given you a complex.

No, it rolls off my back. But you know, Streisand is Streisand, and having her kid stick his tongue out at me is better than nothing at all. Shooting Barbra is always exciting. It was always a challenge when you came into contact with her because you knew you were going to get a run for your money. And you may quote me on that one.

Do you have a certain word or expression you would choose to describe her?

She has the greatest voice that I've ever known. And that it's worth going through anything to be able to listen to that voice.

Have you ever come into contact with Jon Peters?

My experience with Jon Peters was when he was married to Lesley Ann Warren. I've never had any problems with him as far as Streisand. I know that he and Streisand were someplace once and a bunch of photographers came and talked to them and they ran in separate directions and he ran over a fence and hurt himself. Or he hit a photographer. I don't know. There's so much of this stuff, you know. So now what they do is they try to avoid having a confrontation—because they know that when they do they're going to have problems. . . . I guess it has to do with who you're connected with and how they feel at the time. Everyone has his moments.

Is Barbra more difficult to shoot than other superstars or is it simply dependent on her needs?

I think some stars have a certain level they never fall below. And other stars are temperamental and go by their moods.

But is it that Barbra is more moody than other people—or that she is just on such a different level of greatness that she's not even worth comparing?

I don't think you can compare Barbra Streisand to anybody else. Basically, she's always done her own thing. She's always been the kind of person that knows what she wants and gets what she wants. And she now knows from experience how to avoid the confrontations, the public appearances. She doesn't like singing in public that often and she rarely ever does it. Even when she did I LOVE LIBERTY it was taped for her.

She could control what it looked like, do it over if she had to. I guess when you get to a certain level of greatness, taping yourself is very difficult. Certainly never having been in that position I can't speak about what that kind of paranoia is like. Having to reach a level of excellence and never falling below it.

It's admirable that she's taking the risk on YENTL.

Yes—the public does not want to see her in non-singing movies. But she's not going to learn until she does the hard way. They want to see her in musicals, but she wants to be considered as an actress. I'm sure that whenever she does an album she goes through absolute hell, doing things over and over again until she gets it exactly the way she likes it. And since she is who she is, she can afford to take the time and the money to do that. I think people expect it of her. I think her following expects her to be great. Everything she does has to be great. She has to top herself.

The Main Event.
MICHEL PARENTEAU COLLECTION

121

"New York"

RON GALELLA

Known as the most famous paparazzi photographer in the world, Ron Galella's pictures have appeared in nearly every major publication in the world. His photographs of Jacqueline Kennedy Onassis and his numerous court battles with her (he is now forbidden to shoot her) have put him in the media limelight. Mr. Galella has traveled around the world in search of shots, leaving from his home bases in Yonkers, New York, and Los Angeles. He often appears on talk shows and is the author of two books: JACQUELINE and OFF GUARD, a collection of his candid shots of celebrities.

KAREN MOLINE:

When did you begin your career?

RON GALELLA:

I started training in high school, and at the New School for Social Research. I started shooting as an amateur in the U.S. Air Force in Korea from 1951 to 1955. I bought a Rollei to shoot glamour, and began my professional career in the USAF photography school. I shot for the base newspapers, et cetera. Later, after the Air Force, I attended the Art Center School of Design in Los Angeles under the GI Bill.

What do you shoot most often?

Celebrities (movie and television).

Who is your favorite subject?

It used to be Jackie O, but she's nothing but trouble with two trials.

Where are you based?

I'm based in Westchester County [just north of New York City] to cover the New York scene eight months a year. The other four months I spend in Los Angeles.

Where do your photographs appear most often?

My pictures appear in virtually all the major magazines throughout the world.

You are extremely well-known as a paparazzi photographer.

Being a paparazzi has nothing to do with pesty bugs; it has to do with taking pictures in an offguard, spon-

(OPPOSITE) "Broadway for Peace," Philharmonic Hall, January 21, 1968. Galella's favorite photograph.

taneous way to capture people in a natural situation which emphasizes the glamour, and so on. I believe this is more beautiful than the poses.

When did you first shoot Barbra?

January 21, 1968, at the Raffles Club in New York. It also happens to be my favorite photo of Barbra. I also used it in my book OFFGUARD.

How much did you charge for that photo?

I charged the going rate for the magazines, for that time period. For example, the minimum rate for PEO-PLE magazine now (in black and white) is $75. Only inflation has raised my rates.

Did you shoot in black and white or color or both?

I shot more black and white in the past. Now it's fifty-fifty.

What has been your most memorable experience when shooting Barbra?

The most memorable occasion was in a New York boutique shop on East 62nd Street, where I acciden-tally went in to get access for a party at a townhouse with Mia Farrow and André Previn. I thought I could go through the boutique and enter the townhouse through the back. I was surprised to find Barbra and Yves Montand shopping in the boutique. Barbra and Yves were romantically linked and Barbra told me, "Just one picture!" Yves would not pose and left the store alone. I had been photo-graphing Barbra in town while she was filming ON A CLEAR DAY in Central Park and at the Time/Life Plaza

[1969]. Then I had another interesting experience with her. I was waiting in front of Raffles, now called Doubles, at the Sherry Netherland, [an exclusive New York hotel] for Jackie and other celebrities, when Barbra showed up with her agent Lee Solters and a friend. The friend was an unidentified man at the time. I didn't attempt to take her picture, because I had so much on her from ON A CLEAR DAY. To my disappointment, the next day TIME and NEWSWEEK and other magazines were calling for pictures of Barbra and Pierre Trudeau of Canada. That's who the unidentified man was—and I didn't take the picture. I missed it! Lee Solters tells this story time and again to rub it in. I asked Lee, "Why didn't you tell me?" His answer was, "Barbra is my client, not you!"

What was your most embarrassing experience?

That was to see Barbra blow up when a New York fan, Sam Katy, asked her to sign an autograph five

In a New York clothes boutique.

(OPPOSITE) At December 1981 "Woman USA" cocktail benefit.

125

After seeing *Mornings At Seven,*
September 1980.

(OPPOSITE) Another mob scene at
the world premiere of *Funny Lady.*
With Jon Peters, 1975.

times at two locations when they
were filming ON A CLEAR DAY. She
said, "How many times must I sign for
you?!"

How about your best and worst experiences?

My best shoot of Barbra was at a
townhouse where she threw a benefit party for Bella Abzug. It permitted
me to shoot [in] available light and
bounce light. The worst was when I
went to Dolly Parton's opening at the
Roxy and Barbra was there with her
son and she swung her purse at me.

Barbra is not the most cooperative of subjects.

Most of the time Barbra is not cooperative. Even at an event she does
not hold still to pose, [except for] only
a few seconds.

Is she more difficult than the other stars you have worked with?

Yes, she definitely is more difficult than most stars.

Does she project her moods to you when you are shooting her?

Her moods are changeable in a
short time. You've got to catch them.

Where do most of your Barbra photographs appear?

At first the biggest market for
Barbra was the movie and television
magazines, but now I sell more to the
personality magazines, such as PEO-
PLE, US, tabloids, and foreign publications.

What was your initial impression of Barbra?

126

At the party and in the theater for the *Hello Dolly* premiere, December 1969.

With Jon Peters.

My initial impression was that she was a superstar and difficult to photograph because of Lee Solters, her publicity agent. She still is difficult, but Barbra and her agent both know me now. Therefore, she has become easier to shoot.

Has your initial impression changed over the years?

My impression has not changed much over the years. She still is a major superstar that is scarce. She is no longer "hot" as she was in the sixties and seventies.

When was the last time you shot her?

December 23, 1981, at [the] "Woman USA benefit cocktail party" at Diane Von Furstenberg's design studio at 745 Fifth Avenue. Barbra was the guest of honor.

Have you shot her on the sets of any of her movies?

In the summer of 1969, I shot ON A CLEAR DAY YOU CAN SEE FOREVER in Central Park.

How about premieres?

I shot: "Broadway for Peace" at Philharmonic Hall on January 21, 1968 (one of my favorite shots); the FUNNY GIRL birthday party at the Criterion Theater on September 16, 1969; the HELLO DOLLY premiere on December 16, 1969; the FUNNY LADY premiere in Washington D.C. on March 9, 1975; and the A STAR IS BORN premiere party at Tavern on the Green in New York on December 23, 1976.

You must also have shot her at awards ceremonies.

Yes, the Academy Awards in 1969 and 1970; the Golden Globe Awards on January 29, 1977, where she won four awards for A STAR IS BORN; the People's Choice Awards on February 10, 1977; and the 1978 and 1980 Grammy Awards at the Shrine Auditorium.

What do you consider to be her most striking characteristic?

Her voice.

What about her appearance?

Barbra is like Sophia [Loren]; both have unattractive noses and mouths—if looked at separately—but as a whole their faces have beauty.

Do you like how she dresses?

Barbra does dress very fashionably, in striking outfits. See the photographs!

What is the one word or expression you would use to describe Barbra?

New York—her accent and voice.

BOB SCOTT

IMAGES

Jason

One of Jason's frequent appearances during the filming of *Hello Dolly*.

(PAGE 132) With half-sister Roslyn Kind and mother at the Back Lot nightclub in Los Angeles, after Roslyn's singing performance, 1979. (PAGE 133) With Natalie Wood, 1963 and with President Kennedy, 1963.

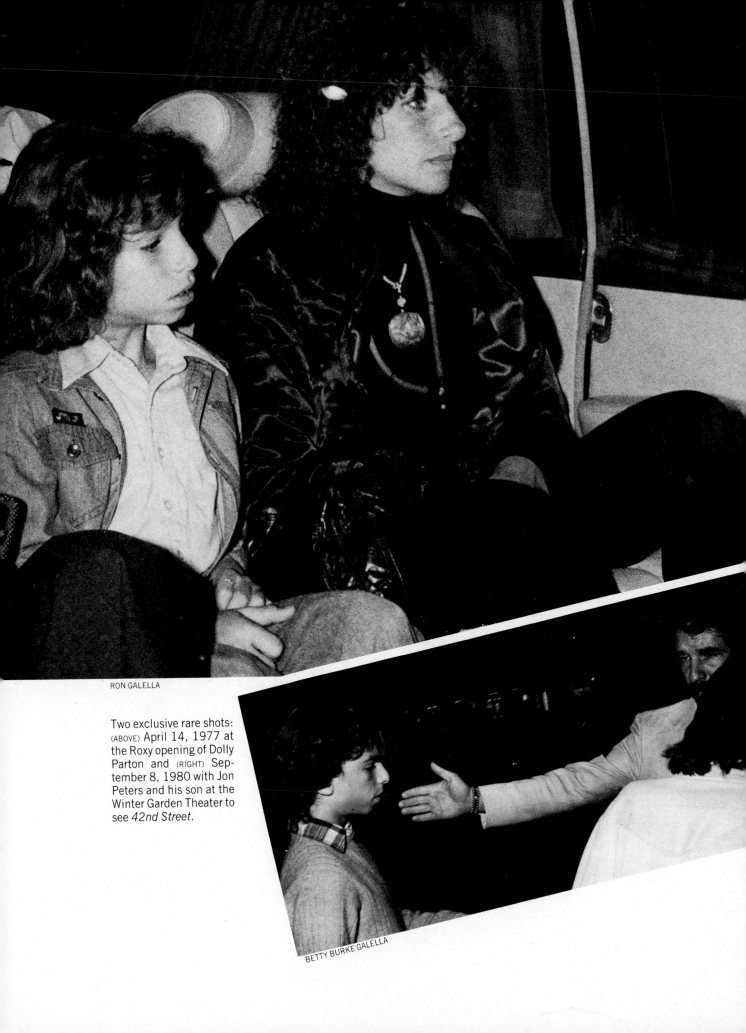

RON GALELLA

Two exclusive rare shots: (ABOVE) April 14, 1977 at the Roxy opening of Dolly Parton and (RIGHT) September 8, 1980 with Jon Peters and his son at the Winter Garden Theater to see *42nd Street*.

BETTY BURKE GALELLA

Co-Stars

The world-famous publicity photograph taken by the renowned Francesco Scavullo for *A Star is Born*. MICHEL PARENTEAU COLLECTION

Scenes from the play *Funny Girl*
with Sidney Chaplin (LEFT) and
the movie (BELOW) with Omar Sharif.
Both men played Nick Arnstein.
MICHEL PARENTEAU COLLECTION

(OPPOSITE TOP) With Ryan O'Neal in *The Main Event.* (OPPOSITE BOTTOM) With Kris Kristofferson in *A Star is Born.* MICHEL PARENTEAU COLLECTION (ABOVE) With Robert Redford in *The Way We Were.* MICHEL PARENTEAU COLLECTION

Friends

(ABOVE) With Canadian Prime Minister Pierre Trudeau, 1970. WIDE WORLD PHOTOS
(LEFT) With President Gerald Ford, 1975. RON GALELLA

(OPPOSITE TOP) With Prince Charles, 1974. WIDE WORLD PHOTOS
(OPPOSITE BOTTOM) Greeting Queen Elizabeth II in 1976 at the premiere of *Funny Lady*. WIDE WORLD PHOTOS

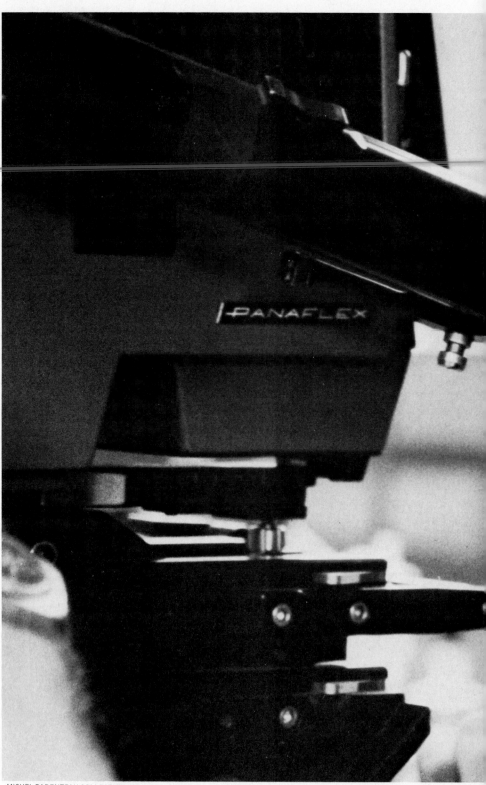

MICHEL PARENTEAU COLLECTION

FRANK TETI

a freelance photographer as well as a representative for other photographers, grew up and still lives in New York's Little Italy. Known around the globe for his shots of celebrities and personalities, he has also photographed the past six presidents of the United States—from Kennedy to Reagan. His favorite photographic subjects are Elizabeth Taylor, Ann-Margret, Robert DeNiro, Robert Redford, Frank Sinatra, Rudolf Nureyev, Bette Midler, and, of course, Barbra Streisand. Interested not only in the "how" and "what," but also in the "why" of photography, Frank Teti chose this unique format to present the photographs of Barbra Streisand that he culled from thousands of different shots. He looks to the work and talent of the late great Sir Cecil Beaton for inspiration. The highlight of Frank's photography career was covering the meeting of President Jimmy Carter and Pope John Paul II at the White House in 1979.

KAREN MOLINE

is a freelance writer and editor based in New York. One of the co-authors of REAR VIEW, her articles have appeared in THE COMPLETE ELVIS, THE COMPLEAT BEATLES, OUI magazine, and NEW YORK ROCKER.